CW00631955

Introduction

Food Finder

Our choice:

INTRODUCTION

Time for Food guides are designed to help you find interesting and enjoyable places to eat in the world's main tourist destinations. Each guide divides the destination into eight areas. Each area has a map, followed by a selection of the restaurants, cafés, bars, pubs and food markets in that area. The aim is to cover the whole spectrum of food establishments, from gourmet temples to humble cafés, plus good food shops or delicatessens where you can buy picnic ingredients or food to cook yourself.

If you are looking for a particular restaurant, regardless of its location, or a particular type of cuisine, you can turn to the Food Finder, starting on page 4. This lists all the establishments reviewed in this guide by name (in alphabetical order) and then by cuisine type.

PRICES

Unlike some guides, we have not wasted space telling you how bad a restaurant is – bad or poor-value restaurants simply do not make it into the guide. Many other guides ask restaurants to pay for their entries, or expect the restaurant to advertise in return for a listing. We do neither of these things: the restaurants and cafés featured here simply represent a selection of places that the author has sampled and enjoyed.

If there is one consistent criterion for inclusion in the guide, it is good

▲ Bridge of Sighs

value. Good value does not, of course, mean cheap necessarily. Food lovers know the difference between a restaurant where the high prices are fully justified by the quality of the ingredients and the excellence of the cooking and presentation of the food, and meretricious establishments where high prices are merely the result of pretentious attitudes.

Some of the restaurants featured here are undeniably expensive if you consume caviar and champagne, but even haute cuisine establishments offer set-price menus (especially at lunchtime) allowing budget diners to enjoy dishes created by top chefs and every bit as good as those on the regular menu. At the same time, some of the eating places listed here might not make it into more conventional food guides, because they are relatively humble cafés or takeaways. Some are deliberately oriented towards tourists, but there is nothing wrong in that: what some guides dismiss as 'tourist traps' may be deservedly popular for providing choice and good value.

FEEDBACK

You may or may not agree with the author's choice – in either case we would like to know about your experiences. Any feedback you give us and any recommendations you make will be followed up, so that you can look forward to seeing your restaurant suggestions in print in the next edition.

Feedback forms have been included at the back of the book and you can e-mail us with comments by writing to: *timeforfood@thomascook.com*. No food guide can keep pace with the changing restaurant scene, as chefs move on, establishments open or close, and menus, opening hours or credit card details change. Let us know what you like or do not like about the restaurants featured here. Tell us if you discover shops, pubs, cafés, bars, restaurants or markets that

you think should go in the guide. Let us know if you discover changes – say to telephone numbers or opening times.

Symbols used in this guide

VISA	Visa accepted
🅾	Diners Club accepted
MasterCard	MasterCard accepted
🍴	Restaurant
🍷	Bar, café or pub
🧺	Shop, market or picnic site
✆	Telephone
⊚	Transport
❷	Numbered red circles relate to the maps at the start of the section

The price indications used in this guide have the following meanings:

❶	budget level
❶❶	typical/average for the destination
❶❶❶	up-market

FOOD FINDER

SHOPS A–Z

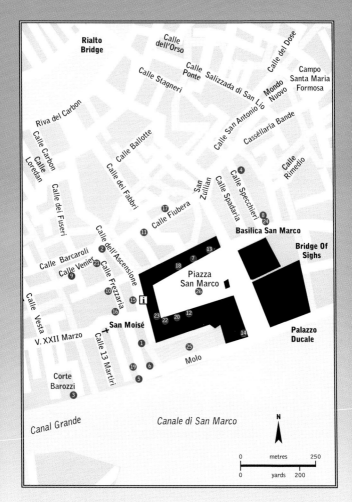

Piazza San Marco

The 'drawing room of Europe', as Napoleon described it, is the focus of Venetian life. The elegant piazza is lined with historical cafés, where you'll have the most expensive cup of coffee in the city – but it will be well worth it. Immediately behind the piazza are many cheap and characterful eating places.

PIAZZA SAN MARCO
Restaurants

Canova ❶

Hotel Luna Baglioni, Calle Valaresso 1243

✆ 520 9550

🚤 Vaporetto Vallaresso

Open: Daily lunch and dinner, closed Aug

Reservations essential

All credit cards accepted

Venetian-International

❸❸❸

In this elegant dining room in an equally elegant hotel, there's an international menu including many Venetian dishes and variations on them. Sea bass fillet is one simple offering, or breast of guinea-fowl en croute with ham and vegetables.

Le Chat Qui Rit ❷

Calle Frezzeria 1131

✆ 522 9086

🚤 Vaporetto Vallaresso

Open: Nov–Aug Sun–Fri 1100–2130, Sep–Oct daily

Reservations not allowed

No credit cards accepted

Venetian

❸

This self-service place is easily the best of the cheap-eat restaurants in central Venice, as you'll see from the lunchtime queues of locals. Get there early, or try it in the evenings. Pizzas, pastas, meat and fish dishes, salads, desserts

… and house wine you help yourself to from the tap.

La Cusina ❸

Hotel Europa and Regina, V. XXII Marzo 2159

✆ 520 0477

🚤 Vaporetto Vallaresso

Open: daily lunch and dinner

Reservations essential

All credit cards accepted

Venetian

❸❸❸

A top class smart restaurant with a terrace overlooking the Grand Canal and the Salute, which is much better than the average hotel restaurant, thanks to the creative versions of local dishes, such as spaghetti in a scorpion fish sauce.

Do Forni ❹

Calle dei Specchieri 468

✆ 523 2148

🚤 Vaporetto San Marco

Open: daily lunch and dinner

Reservations recommended

All credit cards accepted

Venetian-International

❸❸❸

One of the most revered old restaurants in Venice, where the Italian President has dined when visiting. Despite the old-fashioned décor, there are inventive dishes on a

huge menu, such as kidneys cooked in oil, parsley, garlic and black mustard.

Grand Hotel Monaco ❺

Calle Vallaresso 1325

✆ 520 0211

🚤 Vaporetto Vallaresso

Open: daily lunch and dinner

Reservations essential

All credit cards accepted

Venetian-International

❸❸❸

Yet another stunning dining experience, overlooking the Grand Canal (if you can get one of those tables). Try marinated grouper with olives and pinenuts, which is one starter, or duck thighs with rosemary and polenta, one of their established main courses.

Harry's Bar ❻

Calle Vallaresso 1323

✆ 528 5777

Da Toui al "Chat qui rit"

▲ San Marco Basilica and Doge's Palace

<table>
<tr><td>ⓥ Vaporetto Vallaresso</td></tr>
<tr><td>Open: daily 1030–2300</td></tr>
<tr><td>Reservations essential</td></tr>
<tr><td>All credit cards accepted</td></tr>
<tr><td>Venetian</td></tr>
<tr><td>€€€</td></tr>
</table>

A Venice institution (*see pages 16–17*), the bar also has an upstairs restaurant for which you must book. The menu is simple and expensive, with the views and the reputation perhaps counting for more than the food. Seafood ravioli is one typical dish.

Quadri Restaurant ❼

Piazza San Marco

✆ 528 9299

ⓥ Vaporetto San Marco

Open: Wed–Sun lunch and Tue–Sun dinner, closed Mon in winter

Reservations recommended

All credit cards accepted

International

❶❷❸

Above the **Gran Caffè Quadri** (*see page 13*) is an elegant restaurant with stunning views over the piazza. It serves excellent food, too, with dishes such as marinated salmon with fresh coriander or fillet of beef with parmesan and black pepper.

Ristorante Antico Pignolo ❽

Calle dei Specchieri 451

☏ 522 8123

🚤 Vaporetto San Marco

Open: Wed–Mon lunch and dinner

Reservations recommended

All credit cards accepted

Venetian

❶❷❸

Housed in what was once the blacksmith's shop for the Doge's Palace, this venerable place has a reverential atmosphere and one of the best wine cellars in the city. Risotto with black truffles is an example of the type of tasty cuisine on offer.

Trattoria La Colomba ❾

Piscina Frezzeria 1665

☏ 522 1175

🚤 Vaporetto Vallaresso

Open: Thu–Tue lunch and dinner, also open Wed some months

Reservations recommended

All credit cards accepted

Venetian-International

❶❷❸

This smart, relaxed, ancient trattoria has had a recent facelift. Its historical artistic associations are shown in tasting menus such as the Tintoretto. From the main menu, try the seafood risotto or fillet of St Peter's fish with sweet peppers.

Trattoria San Marco ❿

Calle Frezzeria 1610

☏ 528 5242

🚤 Vaporetto Vallaresso

Open: daily for dinner

Reservations unnecessary

💳 💳

Venetian

❶❷

This friendly little family trattoria is worth knowing about if you want decent local food at reasonable prices in this busy area. There are daily specials, and the menu is totally local, with dishes such as liver Venetian-style, lobster, fried squid and plenty of pasta options.

PIAZZA SAN MARCO
Bars, cafés and pubs

Bar Oasi

Calle dei Fabbri 920

☎ 528 5598

🚊 Vaporetto San Marco

Open: daily 0800–2000

No credit cards accepted

€

The kind of unpretentious little snack bar-café that provides good, tasty food at inexpensive prices: the kind of thing that you are often told is impossible in central Venice. At table you can eat pizzas, *gnocchi* and other pastas, have a tiramisu dessert, or from the counter take away a slice of *ciabatta* or *focaccia*.

Caffè Florian ⑫

Piazza San Marco 56

☎ 528 5338

🚊 Vaporetto San Marco

Open: daily 0930–2400, closed Wed in winter

All credit cards accepted

€€€

Founded in 1720 this is *the* café on the piazza.

It's not cheap to sit and sip a glass of Prosecco or a cup of coffee, and you'll pay for the orchestra too, but it's an indulgence you ought to take once while in Venice, perhaps late at night when this becomes an unbeatable romantic setting. Don't miss the intimate old wooden booths inside, too.

Caffè Lavena ⑬

Piazza San Marco 133

☎ 522 4070

🚊 Vaporetto San Marco

Open: daily 0930–0030, closed Tue in winter

All credit cards accepted

€€

Less well-known than its neighbours on the piazza, the Lavena is preferred by many Venetians as it keeps its prices slightly lower to give it an edge on the competition, although you will still pay for the location and the music. Locals also say that

you'll find the best coffee here.

Gran Caffè Chioggia ⑭

Piazza San Marco 8

☎ 528 5011

🚊 Vaporetto San Marco

Open: daily 0800–0100, closed Sun in winter

All credit cards accepted

€€

Slightly off the main piazza and closer to the Grand Canal, this large place emulates the **Florian** (*see above*) and **Quadri** (*see below*) with its acres of outdoor seating and small orchestra or pianist playing. It also does snacks such as sandwiches and pizza slices, as well as ice cream (lemon and vodka?), wine, beer and a range of both teas and coffees.

Gran Caffè Quadri ⑦

Piazza San Marco 120

☎ 522 2105

Snack Bar Oasi

 Vaporetto San Marco

Open: daily 0900–2400, closed Mon in winter

All credit cards accepted

❶❶❶

This is the upstart rival to **Florian** (*see above*), all of fifty years younger. One of its claims to fame is the invention of the powerful coffee drink that became an espresso. It has similar prices and ambience to Florian, with its own small orchestra playing, and it's another delightful spot to savour the piazza. One advantage over Florian is the excellent upstairs restaurant (*see page 10*).

Osteria da Carla ⓯

Corte Contarina 1535

☎ 523 7855

 Vaporetto Vallaresso

Open: Mon–Sat 0700–2030

No credit cards accepted

❶❶

Only a few metres from one of the busiest shopping streets in Venice, the Frezzeria, and yet this place remains undiscovered by most visitors. This little *osteria* has a note outside of the daily fixed menu, which might include pasta with gorgonzola or a seafood salad. Alternatively, just have a snack or enjoy a glass of wine in the totally Venetian atmosphere.

Piccolo Martini ⓰

Calle Frezzeria 1501

☎ 522 8097

 Vaporetto Vallaresso

Open: daily lunch and dinner

All credit cards accepted

❶❶

This friendly and busy bar-café-restaurant on this bustling shopping street is a good retreat for either a drink or a full meal from the typical Venetian menu, covering familiar dishes such as squid in its own ink with polenta, or spaghetti with clams.

Rosa Salva ⓱

Calle Fiubera 951

☎ 521 0544

 Vaporetto San Marco

Open: Mon–Sat all day

No credit cards accepted

❶

One of a chain of Rosa Salva places owned and run by a family of pastry chefs from San Marco. You can stand up at one of the tables and have a coffee or a quick glass of wine, as many locals do, or buy one of the filled rolls to take away. There is also a shop area too, selling all kinds of wicked-looking chocolates and biscuits.

PIAZZA SAN MARCO
Shops, markets and picnic sites

Shops

Galeria San Marco 18

Piazza San Marco 101

☎ 520 1279

◉ Vaporetto San Marco

Open: daily

All credit cards accepted

This is the place to come if you want to buy a piece of artwork by Dali, Picasso or Chagall, and other contemporary artists. Many of them have produced striking glasses and vases, and if you have several million lire to spare you can have a giant bunch of grapes as a table decoration.

Industrie Veneziane 19

Calle Vallaresso 1320

☎ 523 0509

◉ Vaporetto Vallaresso

Open: daily, closed Mon am

All credit cards accepted

A good range of glassware from the shop that provides the carafes to **Harry's Bar** (*see pages 16–17*). Their stock ranges from cheap wineglasses through to expensive traditional designs in bright blues, reds and greens, with barley-sugar stems.

Jesurum 20

Piazza San Marco 60–1

☎ 522 9864

◉ Vaporetto San Marco

Open: daily

All credit cards accepted

A century-old lace shop on the piazza, where prices are high but the very best quality is guaranteed. There are some very delicate, almost filigree, tablecloths and place mats available, far too good for everyday use but superb for a special occasion. But there are also cheaper, more robust items, too.

Marco Polo International 21

Calle Frezzeria 1644

☎ 522 9295

◉ Vaporetto Vallaresso

Open: daily

All credit cards accepted

One of the best-stocked glass shops in Venice, with a great variety of items on display on two floors. As well as whimsical little Murano knick-knacks, there are creations by artists working in glass, which are exclusive to the shop. Several shelves are filled with drinking glasses, mainly far more refined and tasteful than most on display in the city, and you can even order a table made completely of glass and have it shipped home to you ... at a price!

Martinuzzi 22

Piazza San Marco 67A

☎ 522 5068

◉ Vaporetto San Marco

Open: daily, closed 1230–1500 in winter

All credit cards accepted

Sophisticated shop selling both lace and ceramics, and well worth investigating if you want something colourful but tasteful for the kitchen or the dining table. There are some exquisite candles

▲ Campanile

in bright yellow, dinner plates decorated with lemons and other food designs, with matching yellow napkins. Vases, water jugs and wine-glasses are on sale too, as well as a range of lace tablecloths and tablemats.

Pauly and Co 23

Piazza San Marco 73–7

✆ 523 5484

🚤 Vaporetto San Marco

Open: daily

All credit cards accepted

A small retail shop for the renowned Pauly glassmakers. This is more for show on the piazza, but, although small, it does have some good examples of their delicate wineglasses, as well as more elaborate water jugs and vases.

Venini 24

Piazzetta Leoncini 314

✆ 522 4045

🚤 Vaporetto San Zaccaria

Open: Tue–Sat, closed 1230–1530

All credit cards accepted

Extremely stylish and modern glass shop, which ought not to be lumped in with those souvenir shops selling brash Murano glass-ware. The approach here is minimalist and gallery-like. The pieces certainly are works of art, including glass plates in pastel colours that would set off any meal, beautiful water jugs and vases, and

even that chandelier you've always wanted for the dining room!

Vetri d'Arte 13

Piazza San Marco 140

✆ 520 0205

🚤 Vaporetto Vallaresso

Open: daily

All credit cards accepted

A slightly more up-market glass shop, in this touristy area where glass shops are more easily found than food shops. This has a good line in elaborate Murano glass goblets, for those whose taste is for the ornate rather than the simple. Some, for example, have bases the shape of seahorses, in vivid colours such as bright blue and gold … or just plain gold if you prefer.

Picnic sites

Giardinetti Reali 25

🚤 Vaporetto San Marco

This little oasis of greenery is right behind the various San Marco

waterbus, watertaxi and gondola stops, and the row of souvenir stalls that lines the front. It offers a little respite from the bustle, with benches, trees and bushes, and it is often surprisingly quiet. The little gardens were created in the early 19th century by a nephew of Napoleon to provide him with a pleasant view from his palace.

Piazza San Marco 26

🚤 Vaporetto San Marco

It might seem odd to suggest Venice's main piazza as a picnic spot, but if you go to the western end, the opposite end from the basilica, there are steps running along outside the Museo Correr where lots of people do sit and soak up the sunshine and the view. Can there be any better place in Venice to eat your picnic than 'the most elegant drawing room in Europe', as Napoleon described it?

Harry's Bar

Bringing Boston to Venice

Harry's Bar seems to have been a feature of Venice for almost as long as the Doge's Palace, and while there are several other Harry's Bars in various cities around the world this is the original. So who was Harry? **Harry Pickering** was a wealthy Boston businessman who felt that despite the high number of bars in Venice, there wasn't one which was just the way he liked them, so he wanted to open his own.

At the same time as this, a hotel barman named **Giuseppe Cipriani** was also keen to open a bar of his own, and had found the ideal location: a disused storeroom and rope factory right by the Grand Canal and very close to the Piazza San Marco. So when Harry met Giuseppe, Harry's Bar was born using Pickering's money and Cipriani's bar expertise. The bar was quickly successful and Cipriani was soon able to repay the money, making the bar his own, and Pickering was happy he had somewhere he really liked to drink. Cipriani was obviously an enterprising guy, as not long after the bar was opened he came up with an idea for a cocktail, the **Bellini**, and that too was successful – so much so that they are still in demand today, with the recipe (of course) a closely guarded secret. The basic ingredients are fresh white peach juice and the local sparkling wine, Prosecco. The true version of the drink can therefore be made only during the season for white peaches, which runs from the early

▲ Harry's Bar

summer through to October, and strictly speaking the true version can only be found in Harry's Bar, where making a Bellini involves lots of showmanship and pouring the mixture back and forward between several different glasses to get the right amount of fizz. The Bellini in its turn spawned other similar cocktails, combining Prosecco with other ingredients including orange juice, grape juice, strawberry juice, raspberry juice and other options, all of them refreshing fizzy drinks.

> **... making a Bellini involves lots of showmanship and pouring the mixture back and forward between several different glasses to get the right amount of fizz ...**

Harry's Bar has attracted numerous celebrities over the years, including movie stars such as **Humphrey Bogart** and **Lauren Bacall**, singer **Frank Sinatra**, the British wartime leader **Sir Winston Churchill**, author **Gore Vidal** and more recently celebrities such as **Madonna** and **Woody Allen**. Allen is a regular visitor to Venice and to Harry's Bar, as not only has he filmed in the city, he also likes to attend the autumn Film Festival. At one time in 1935 no less than three **European kings** used to meet in Harry's regularly: King Paul of Greece, King Alfonso of Spain and King Peter of Yugoslavia.

Perhaps the most notable name associated with Harry's Bar is the American writer **Ernest Hemingway**, who came up with a drink rather more potent than the Bellini: the **Montgomery**. This was named after Field-Marshall Montgomery of Alamein, and mixed 15 measures of gin with just one of vermouth. That was the same ratio by which the Allied troops outnumbered the Germans when they were being driven out of Italy.

In the 1950s Giuseppe Cipriani's inventive mind was at work again, this time coming up with carpaccio, the dish made primarily from fine slivers of raw beef (*see recipe on pages 94–5*). If you want to sample this you'll have to dine in the upstairs restaurant, which has fine views across the Grand Canal to the church of Santa Maria della Salute on Giudecca. Check the prices first, though, as this is the kind of place where most visitors could only afford the view. Many settle for a quick peek inside, surprised to find that the place looks quite ordinary, and downstairs the drinkers are shielded from the passers-by and the views by frosted glass. No doubt the celebrities prefer it that way, although you have far more chance of spotting a gondola-load of American or Japanese tourists, hoping to spot a celebrity while they sip their Bellinis.

The present owner and main host at Harry's is the son of the founder, Arrigo Cipriani. Arrigo is the Italian version of Harry, causing Arrigo to quip that he is the only person in the world named after a bar.

For further details see page 9.

San Marco

The San Marco district is the centre of Venice for most visitors, caught in the loop of the Grand Canal and including the majority of the city's main attractions. For the food lover it is a goldmine, as it also includes several of the city's finest restaurants, plus lively bars and cafés.

SAN MARCO
Restaurants

Antico Martini ❶

Campo San Fantin 1983

☏ 522 4121

🚏 Vaporetto San Marco or Santa Maria del Giglio

Open: Thu–Mon lunch and dinner and Wed dinner

Reservations recommended

All credit cards accepted

Venetian-International

❸❸❸

An elegant and formal restaurant offering some of the best food in Venice, with service to match. The wine list runs to 350 labels and dishes include sea scallops with basil and a mouth-watering freshly made polenta, or *tagliolini* with asparagus.

Le Bistrot de Venise ❷

Calle dei Fabbri 4685

☏ 523 6651

🚏 Vaporetto Rialto

Open: daily until 0100

Reservations unnecessary

All credit cards accepted

Venetian-French

❸❸

Excellent and bustling French-style bistro with a late 19th-century feel. It often has live events and publishes a leaflet with the details. The food mixes local cuisine (some from old recipes) and French. Try goby and eel risotto or just a pizza.

La Caravella ❸

Hotel Saturnia, Calle Larga XXII Marzo 2398

☏ 520 8901

🚏 Vaporetto San Marco

Open: daily lunch and dinner

Reservations recommended

All credit cards accepted

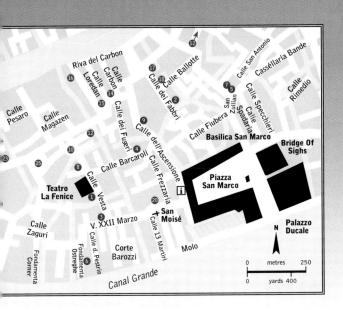

▲ Antico Martini

International

This elegant restaurant has three dining rooms and a hidden courtyard, and is one of the best hotel restaurants in Venice. Creamed lobster soup and risotto made with shrimps and early vegetables are just two of the tempting dishes.

Da Ivo ❹

Calle dei Fuseri 1809

☎ 528 5004

🚊 Vaporetto San Marco

Open: Mon–Sat lunch and dinner, closed most of Jan

Reservations essential

All credit cards accepted

▲ Ristorante da Raffaele

Italian

Traditional, romantic and candlelit, the long-established Da Ivo exudes charm and hospitality. The Tuscan owner mixes Tuscan and Venetian cuisine: Florentine steak, Piedmont truffles and *tagliolini* with mullet roe are just some of the options.

Ristorante Al Conte Pescaor ❺

Piscina San Zulian 544

☎ 522 1483

🚊 Vaporetto San Marco or Rialto

Open: daily lunch and dinner, closed Sun in Jan

Reservations unnecessary

All credit cards accepted

Venetian

Hidden behind San Marco is this old-fashioned restaurant with a historically protected interior and some casual outdoor dining. The seafood is good, as is the pasta. Combine the two in *gnocchi* with crab and rocket or *tagliolini* with salmon.

Ristorante da Raffaele ❻

Calle Larga XXII Marzo 2347

☎ 523 2317

🚊 Vaporetto San Marco or Santa Maria del Giglio

Open: Fri–Wed lunch and dinner, closed mid-Dec–mid-Feb

Reservations recommended

All credit cards accepted

Italian

The relaxed canalside tables right by where gondolas are moored belie the dramatic old interior with swords and chandeliers, and hanging pots and pans. The dishes are good but straightforward: scampi, squid, pasta and fresh fish.

Sempione ❼

Ponte Beretteri 578

☎ 522 6022

🚊 Vaporetto Rialto

Open: daily lunch and dinner

Reservations recommended

All credit cards accepted

Venetian

●●

An inexpensive place in a 15th-century building overlooking a canal, the Sempione has been in business for almost a century and serves simple but pleasing dishes such as grilled tuna, salmon or sea bass, in a relaxed atmosphere.

Taverna La Fenice ⑧

Campiello de la Fenice 1938

∅ 522 3856

🚤 Vaporetto San Marco

Open: May–July daily lunch and dinner, closed Aug–Apr Sun lunch and all day Mon and second week in Jan

Reservations unnecessary

All credit cards accepted

Venetian

●●

Sea bass with cream and capers, or scallops and asparagus are two representative dishes in this restaurant which first opened in 1907 alongside the now-burned Fenice opera house. The interior is ornate, but the outdoor seating casual.

▲ Terrazza Goldoni

Terrazza Goldoni ⑨

Calle Goldoni 4488

∅ 522 4168

🚤 Vaporetto San Marco

Open: daily lunch and dinner

Reservations unnecessary

All credit cards accepted

Italian

●●●

An up-market restaurant in the heart of the city surrounded by greenery and with a hushed atmosphere enhanced by piano music. The extensive menu ranges through the day's catch simply grilled, hearty pepper steaks or *tagli-olini* with salmon.

Vini da Arturo ⑩

Calle degli Assassini 3656

∅ 528 6974

🚤 Vaporetto San Marco or Rialto

Open: Mon–Sat lunch and dinner, closed Aug

Reservations recommended

No credit cards accepted

Venetian

●●

This tiny place is as homely as it can get, but the simple dishes are made with great care and fine ingredients: scallops in lemon or in white wine, but beef rather than fish is the speciality here.

SAN MARCO
Bars, cafés and pubs

Caffè Brasolia ⑩

Rio Tera dei Assassini 3658A

✆ 528 7896

Vaporetto Sant' Angelo

Open: Mon–Sat lunch and dinner

No credit cards accepted

This easy-going small café has a neighbourly feel to it, with a few tables outside on a quiet street, and more inside, where people take a break from shopping over a cup of coffee or a glass of beer, and snack on sandwiches and pastries while having a gossip.

Osteria agli Assassini ⑪

Rio Tera dei Assassini 3695

✆ 528 7986

Vaporetto Sant' Angelo

Open: Mon–Fri lunch and evenings, closed two weeks in Aug

No credit cards accepted

Tiny *osteria* in a backstreet with a few coveted tables outside, from where you can watch the gondolas drift by along the canal at the end of the dead-end street. The brick walls and wooden bar make for a cosy interior, where you can get a good range of wines by the glass along with snacks and some more substantial dishes.

Osteria alla Botte ⑫

Calle de la Bissa 5482

✆ 520 9775

Vaporetto Rialto

Open: Fri–Wed am and evening, closed July and Christmas

No credit cards accepted

If you can find this tiny bar down a maze of backstreets off the busy Campo San Bartolomeo then you deserve a drink – just pray you can get to the busy bar and order one. It's an immensely popular old-fashioned yet fashionable place serving wine, *cicchetti* or, in the rear room, slightly bigger meals.

▲ Al Teatro

Osteria alle Botteghe ⑬

Calle delle Botteghe 3454

✆ 522 8181

Vaporetto Accademia

Open: daily from 1000

No credit cards accepted

Just fifty yards from the more expensive cafés that surround the Campo San Stefano is this cheaper option. The Botteghe is a fairly modern *osteria* but with a traditional look to it, with its ceiling of wooden beams and walls of wood and brickwork. It serves the usual range of beers, wines, hot drinks and soft drinks, as well as snacks and sandwiches to eat at one of the tables, standing up at the bar, or take away with you.

Rosa Salva ⑭

Campo San Luca 4589

✆ 522 5385

Vaporetto Rialto

Open: Mon–Sat all day

No credit cards accepted

One of a small chain of coffeeshops-cum-bars-cum-food-stores, Rosa Salva is the kind of place you can call in for a quick restorative cup

of coffee, drunk standing up, or a glass of wine and a lunchtime sandwich, or where you can buy a delicious cake or box of Venetian chocolates.

Al Teatro

Campo San Fantin 1916

✆ 522 1052

🚤 Vaporetto Sant' Angelo

Open: Tue–Sun all day

💳💳 VISA

The food on offer in this combination of bar, brasserie and restaurant, with lots of outdoor seating on the Campo San Fantin, can be as costly as boiled lobster in mayonnaise, or as cheap as a pizza. The bar inside with its long curving counter really buzzes too.

Vino Vino ❶

Valle del Cafetier 2007A

✆ 523 7027

🚤 Vaporetto Santa Maria del Giglio

Open: Wed–Mon all day

All credit cards accepted

This characterful little wine bar is next to, and owned by, the **Antico Martini** restaurant (*see page 18*). The restaurant kitchens also provide the food, so although they are simple nibbles such as rice salad or sardines in *saor* (sweet-and-sour sauce), they are all impeccably prepared with the freshest of ingredients. Vino Vino also has a huge range of wines available by the glass or bottle, with bottles costing as

▲ Vino Vino

little or as much as you desire. There's a great choice of grappas too.

Vitae ❶

Calle Sant' Antonio

✆ 520 5205

🚤 Vaporetto Rialto

Open: Mon–Sat all day

No credit cards accepted

This tiny café-bar in a cul-de-sac is a hangout for fashionable young Venetians, and the kind of place where conversation often has to be shouted over the music and other conversations. A place to be seen with a cocktail or a late-night grappa, rather than for a relaxed chat.

Al Volto ❶

Calle Cavalli 4081

✆ 522 8945

🚤 Vaporetto Rialto

Open: Mon–Sat 1000–1430, 1700–2230

No credit cards accepted

Opened in 1936, this terrific wine bar not far from the Rialto is a million miles from the touristy face of the city. It's the kind of place where locals walk in and their favoured drink is on the counter before they reach it. The counter also has a range of bar snacks such as squid, ham, cheeses and sardines.

SAN MARCO
Shops, markets and picnic sites

Shops

Ceramiche Volmente

Calle delle Botteghe 3455
☏ 522 9943
⊕ Vaporetto Accademia
Open: daily 0900–2000
All credit cards accepted

A small but good selection of ceramics in bold and unusual designs, with classical leanings. In addition to the usual bowls, plates and cups, there are everyday kitchen objects such as lemon-squeezers, butter dishes and soup tureens. There are some unusually designed clocks for the kitchen wall too.

Domus

Calle dei Fabbri 4746
☏ 522 6259
⊕ Vaporetto Rialto
Open: daily
All credit cards accepted

A huge stock of kitchenware, which is more conventional than **Epicentro** (*see below*), with dinner services, coffeemakers, ceramics, cutlery, vases, glasses and every kind of kitchen implement, mostly in stylish Italian designs.

Epicentro

Calle dei Fabbri 932
☏ 522 6864
⊕ Vaporetto Rialto
Open: daily
All credit cards accepted

A funky little kitchen-ware shop with lots of stock in bright primary colours, which will definitely bring a Mediterranean cheerfulness to any kitchen anywhere. Perhaps a surreal clock for the kitchen wall, or a lemon-squeezer designed by Philippe Starck, or one featuring Flash Gordon? It's that kind of place.

Galleria Marina Barovier

Salizzada San Samuele 3216
☏ 523 6748
⊕ Vaporetto San Samuele
Open: Mon–Sat
All credit cards accepted

For those who prefer their table glassware to be rather more sophisticated than the frequently garish Murano look, this shop-gallery stocks some of the finest examples of work by Italy's leading glass sculptors. Some chandeliers and other large items run into millions of lira, but you can buy more affordable one-off wineglasses or fruit bowls in tasteful pastel colours or plain glass that is exquisitely styled.

L'Isola

Campo San Moisé 1468
☏ 523 1973
⊕ Vaporetto San Marco
Open: daily 0900–1300, 1530–1930
All credit cards accepted

Look for the name of Carlo Moretti in the window, the glassmaker whose stunning and individual work is on sale here. There are beautiful crystal glasses, sets of wineglasses, handmade individual long-stemmed glasses in elaborate designs, plates in pastel patterns and in bold primary colours.

Marchini

Ponte San Maurizio 2769
☏ 522 9109
⊕ Vaporetto Santa Maria del Giglio
Open: Wed–Mon all day
All credit cards accepted

One of the best pastry and cake shops in Venice, its windows invariably besieged by tourists tempted by the mouth-watering displays of cakes large and small, pastries and especially chocolates. There are plain chocolates, chocolates with every filling imaginable, and numerous novelty chocolates, some in the shape of carnival masks and some showing men and women performing acts that are enough to make the chocolate melt.

Materia Prima 22

Piscina San Samuele 3436

✆ 523 3282

🚤 Vaporetto San Samuele

Open: Mon–Sat 1000–1230, 1600–1930

All credit cards accepted

An exquisite collection of arts and crafts with a strong oriental emphasis, so there are tiny teapots, some with sets of cups on a tray, bowls, chopsticks, plates, but other delightful and tasteful objects too, such as wineglasses and candles. Unusual, stylish and very original.

Rigattieri 23

Calle Frati 3532/36

✆ 523 1081

🚤 Vaporetto Sant' Angelo

Open: Mon–Sat 0900–2000, closed lunch

All credit cards accepted

A large collection of good-quality ceramics, silver and glassware, plus silver tea services and trays, canteens of cutlery, dinner sets, beautiful tiny tea cups and lovely wineglasses, vases and jugs. All can be shipped anywhere in the world.

> Picnic sites

Campo San Stefano 24

🚤 Vaporetto Sant' Angelo

The Campo San Stefano is impressively huge and is one of the city's focal points. The wide open centre is surrounded by cafés and restaurants, but if you want a cheaper snack then you could perch beneath the statue or by one of the two old wells and tuck into some food in one of the most striking *campos* in Venice.

Campo Sant' Angelo 25

🚤 Vaporetto Sant' Angelo

This small *campo* is the perfect picnic spot in this area, with several benches at one end that have small tables between them. They are even covered by a canopy to provide some shade, and hence are very popular with the local people. There are cafés all around, and also a public toilet in one corner of the *campo*, accessed by a pay-turnstile.

▲ Campo San Stefano

Business dining

Dining to impress

Venice is not a major business centre like Rome or Milan, as its main business is tourism and the only meetings needed here are to discuss how to keep the numbers down to a manageable level. The only industry in the city is obviously small-scale, with the major industries kept well outside the lagoon on the mainland, making Venice itself not the most convenient place for businessmen to meet. It also means that there are few places with small private rooms, if your business is confidential, as the private rooms available are mostly large ones, to cater for family functions rather than business lunches or dinners.

Nevertheless, if you do have business to conduct in Venice and want to make sure you impress your colleagues with a good meal, and show you have a knowledge of the city's best restaurants, there are several places that would make good choices. To begin with, could anything beat taking the **Hotel Cipriani**'s private boat from the jetty near San Marco and whisking a business colleague over to dine in the restaurant in this luxury hotel on Giudecca (*see page 56*)? It is one of the few restaurants in Venice which requires men to wear a jacket and tie, and where children under the age of six are not allowed, giving an indication of the atmosphere and the clientele. If the weather is fine there are tables on the lovely terrace overlooking the lagoon, and the food is good enough to make it one of the best restaurants in Venice. Pastas are freshly made and aside from the best tiramisu you will ever taste, a real treat would be to come here in the autumn and have white truffles in a champagne risotto.

▲ Hotel Cipriani

In the city itself, the **Antico Martini** (*see page 18*) has been on its site by the Fenice for almost 300 years, and has been in the hands of the same family now for three generations. The owner, Emilio Baldi, makes a courteous host, escorting people to their tables and chatting affably as if everyone were an old friend. His staff provide impeccable service and the food justifies many people's view that this is the best restaurant in Venice. One of the secrets is using the best possible ingredients, such as extra-virgin olive oil, which is never re-used. The Antico Martini also has one of the best wine lists in Venice, and afterwards you can relax in the sophisticated **Piano Bar**, which is open till late.

If you are on a limitless expense account then anyone would be impressed by a meal at **Harry's Bar** (*see pages 16 and 17*). Begin with a Bellini in the bar where the drink was invented, be charmed by the gregarious owner Arrigo Cipriani, and if you're wise you'll have booked ahead and asked for a table with a view over the Grand Canal.

The best views combined with the best meals cannot fail to impress, and another perfect spot for doing this is by reserving one of the tables at the **Quadri Restaurant** (*see page 10*) which has views over the Piazza San Marco. This has to be one of the best views in Europe, and is fortunately matched by

top-quality service and cuisine. On the other hand, the view from the rooftop **Ristorante Terrazza** at the **Danieli Hotel** (*see page 40*) is also pretty impressive, looking out across the San Marco Canal (which is what the Grand Canal becomes when it widens out) to the skyline of the little island of San Giorgio Maggiore. Arrange to be having your pre-dinner drinks as the sun is going down and hopefully casting a golden glow on the buildings.

This has to be one of the best views in Europe, and is fortunately matched by top-quality service and cuisine.

If the occasion demands a more informal setting, then **Da Ivo** (*see page 20*) might provide the answer. Just behind Piazza San Marco and alongside a canal, you could, if you wished, go the whole Venice hog and arrange to arrive here by gondola, as these can moor right outside. Inside, the décor is old-fashioned, the atmosphere lively and the service friendly, the perfect place for a more relaxed business meeting.

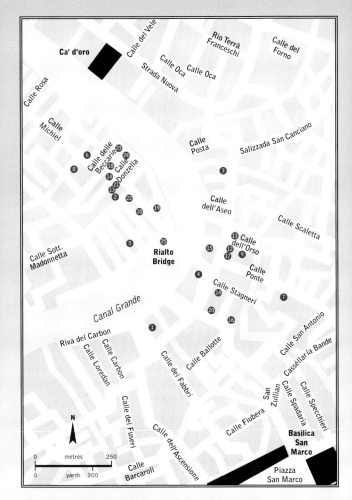

Around the Rialto Bridge

The area around the Rialto Bridge is an especially busy one as it is favoured by tourists and locals alike, with many locals coming to the excellent fish and vegetable markets. Tourists congregate around the bridge, the nearby souvenir shops and alongside the Grand Canal, but in the warren of backstreets are some of the best eating places in the city.

Antica Carbonera ①

Calle Bembo 4648

☎ 522 5479

🚤 Vaporetto Rialto

Open: daily for lunch and dinner, closed Thu and Sun but varies

Reservations unnecessary

All credit cards accepted

Venetian

€€

A charming and simple old restaurant, with private booths lining each side of the main room. There's courteous service of plain but well-prepared Venetian dishes, including spider-crab, steak with *foie gras* or liver Venetian-style. Homemade cakes for dessert.

Antico Dolo ②

Ruga Vecchia San Giovanni 778

☎ 522 6546

🚤 Vaporetto Rialto

Open: Mon-Sat lunch and dinner, closed two weeks in Aug

Reservations recommended

💳 💳 American Express

Venetian

€€

A bright and busy *osteria* with old photos lining the walls and exceptionally good food. If you are hungry, try the mixed plate of appetisers which might include octopus with celery and *sarde* (sardines) in *saor* (sweet-and-sour sauce). Boiled tripe is a house speciality.

Fiaschetteria Toscana ③

Salizzada San Giovanni Crisostomo 5719

☎ 528 5281

🚤 Vaporetto Rialto

Open: Wed-Mon lunch and dinner, closed the week after the carnival and two weeks in June-July

Reservations recommended

All credit cards accepted

Venetian

€€€

Despite the Tuscan name, this serves some of the best Venetian food in the city. Try

RISTORANTE "al graspo de ua"

Reservations recommended

 American Express

Seafood-Venetian

€€

This is the unpretentious old place that locals head for while tourists sit in the restaurants beside the Grand Canal fifty metres away. Aim to dine early in the plain but busy dining room, where fresh seafood is always the best option.

Ai Poste Vecie ❻

Pesceria Rialto 1608

✆ 721 822

🚤 Vaporetto Rialto

Open: Thu–Mon and Tue lunch

Reservations unnecessary

All credit cards accepted

Seafood

€€€

There has been a restaurant here by the fish market since the 16th century, and today's up-market place serves the best of the day's catch, but has meat and vegetarian pasta dishes too. Try the fried tiny crabs or stewed eel.

Ristorante Marco Polo ❼

Salizzada San Lio 5571

✆ 523 5018

🚤 Vaporetto Rialto

Open: daily lunch and dinner

Reservations unnecessary

All credit cards accepted

Italian

€€

The Marco Polo is a simple streetside

their perfect risotto with seasonal vegetables, or *tagliolini* with spidercrab. Leave room for their homemade desserts and enjoy the exceptional wine list.

Al Graspo de Ua ❹

Calle dei Bombaseri 5094A

✆ 520 0150/522 3647

🚤 Vaporetto Rialto

Open: Wed–Sun lunch and dinner, closed two weeks mid-Jan

Reservations recommended

All credit cards accepted

Seafood-Venetian

€€€

This is one of the best seafood restaurants in Venice, in smart-casual style, with many distinguished customers. Dishes include simple but well-prepared options such as fried scampi and calamari in a tartare salsa, and fresh salmon with herbs.

Alla Madonna ❺

Calle della Madonna 594

✆ 522 3824

🚤 Vaporetto Rialto

Open: Thu–Tue lunch and dinner, closed two weeks in Jan/Feb and two weeks in Aug

restaurant, with a few outdoor tables, serving up good medium-priced food from a typical menu that includes dishes such as liver Venetian-style, mixed fried fish and a tasty tiramisu dessert.

Do Spade ⑧

Calle do Spade 860

✆ 521 0574

🚤 Vaporetto Rialto

Open: Mon–Sat lunch and dinner, closed Thu dinner

Reservations unnecessary

No credit cards accepted

Venetian

€

This classic old *osteria* is all wood-panels, barrels and blackboards, and the menu is vast. Starters include pasta with pumpkin or for main course there are delights such as roast suckling pig or Venetian codfish with polenta.

Al Tempio del Paradiso ⑨

Calle dell'Orso 5495

✆ 522 4673

🚤 Vaporetto Rialto

Open: Tue–Sun lunch and dinner

Reservations unnecessary

💳 💳 American Express

Chinese

€

Hidden down an alley behind Campo San Bartolomeo is this pleasant Chinese restaurant whose extensive and reasonably-priced menu includes such dishes as bamboo and Chinese mushrooms, Szechuan-style pork and many vegetarian options. Chinese beer makes the perfect accompaniment.

Tian Jin ⑩

Ruga Rialto 649

✆ 520 4603

Ristorante
MARCO POLO

🚤 Vaporetto Rialto

Open: daily 1030–2400

Reservations unnecessary

All credit cards accepted

Chinese

€

This smart but inexpensive Chinese restaurant has the usual extensive menu for those wanting a change from Italian food. Begin with a hot-and-sour soup, move on to sweet-and-sour spare ribs, and how about a dessert of fried ice cream?

AROUND THE RIALTO BRIDGE
Bars, cafés and pubs

Bacaro Jazz ⑪

Salizada del Fontego dei
Tedeschi 5546

✆ 528 5249

🚤 Vaporetto Rialto

Open: Thu–Tue 1100–0200

No credit cards accepted

New music bar-*bacaro*
with a loud but lazy
atmosphere, with a
happy hour that lasts
from 1400 until 1900
every day and live
music late at night.
There are plenty of
beers to choose from,
plus wines of course,
and if you fancy some
food too there are either
tapas-like bar snacks or
a limited but cheap
two-course menu.

Alla Botte ⑫

Calle de la Bissa 5482

✆ 520 9775

🚤 Vaporetto Rialto

Open: Sun–Fri 0900–1530,
1630–2330

No credit cards accepted

This *osteria* with good
food is down a back
alley that you probably
wouldn't venture along
in any other city, but in
Venice they are per-
fectly safe and also con-
ceal some of the most
atmospheric bars
around. Try an octopus
starter or a plate of
lasagne, or liver
Venetian-style if you
want a more substantial

meal … or just enjoy
the wine and the buzz.

Cantina all' Arco ⑬

Calle dell' Ochialer 436

✆ 520 5666

🚤 Vaporetto Rialto

Open: Mon–Sat 0800–1600,
Mon–Fri 1830–2200

No credit cards accepted

Half a dozen outside
tables mark this down-
to-earth *osteria*, though
at mealtimes the small
interior is crammed with
market traders, shoppers
and a few adventurous
tourists snapping up the
above-average bar
snacks such as wild
boar *prosciutto*, sar-
dines, anchovies or
calamari.

Devil's Forest Bar ⑭

Calle Stagneri 5185

✆ 520 0623

🚤 Vaporetto Rialto

Open: Tue–Sun all day

No credit cards accepted

If you can imagine such
a thing as a Venetian
Irish bar then this is it.
Guinness and other
beers, and bar games
such as darts, all mingle
happily with two simple
fixed-price menus which
might include the local
St Peter's fish and a
choice of pastas.

Do Mori ⑬

Calle do Mori 429

✆ 522 5401

🚤 Vaporetto Rialto

Open: Mon–Sat 0900–1300
and 1700–2000, closed Wed
pm

No credit cards accepted

This bar has been in
business since 1462, so
it ought to have got
things right by now. It
is one of the most
atmospheric of Venice's
old *bacari*: no-frills
wine bars which serve
snacks or meals. Choose
from 20 bar snacks, or
wine from the barrels,
though there are over
350 wines on offer in
all. No seating but lots
of bonhomie from the
market traders.

Osteria ai do Ladroni ⑮

Ramo del Fontego dei
Tedeschi 5362

✆ 522 7741

🚤 Vaporetto Rialto

Open: Mon–Sat dinner

No credit cards accepted

A very ordinary-looking
but exceptionally char-
acterful *osteria*, barely
fifty metres from the
Rialto Bridge but a hun-
dred miles from its
tourist razzamatazz. You
can have simple sand-
wiches and snacks at
the bar or grab a table
and try the pasta and
bean soup or grilled fish
and a salad.

Da Pinto ❻

Campo de la Becarie 367

✆ 522 4599

◉ Vaporetto Rialto

Open: Tue–Sun 0730–1430, 1800–2030

No credit cards accepted

Café-bar in a great spot on the Campo de la Becarie, which is small and has its own intimate atmosphere, but is busy with shoppers coming and going to the nearby markets, and tourists who have ventured a little bit further from the Rialto Bridge area. A lovely place to linger over coffee or something a bit stronger.

Rosa Salva ❶❻

Merceria San Salvador 5020

✆ 522 7934

◉ Vaporetto Rialto

Open: Mon–Sat

No credit cards accepted

One of a small chain of shops owned by a local family of pastry chefs, this is also a café-bar where you can stand up and have a quick coffee or glass of wine, and then browse among the tempting goodies such as chocolates and grappa to take away.

Rosticceria ❶❼

Calle de la Bissa 5424

✆ 522 3569

◉ Vaporetto Rialto

Open: Tue–Sun

All credit cards accepted

There's something for everyone here, as downstairs is a bar, café, pizza parlour, takeaway and food and wine shop, and upstairs if you want a sit-down meal is a slightly more formal eating area serving such dishes as seafood risotto.

Ai Rusteghi ❶❶

Calle de la Bissa 5529

✆ 523 2205

◉ Vaporetto Rialto

Open: Mon–Sat from 0900

No credit cards accepted

Another of Venice's great little backstreet bars, which would be full if it had two dozen people inside it. It's hard to find, which adds to the attraction as few tourists get here. The fairly plain bar has filled rolls and sandwiches to eat there or to take away, or grab one of the few tables and relax with a coffee or a beer and see that increasingly elusive thing, the *real* Venice.

▲ Rialto Bridge

AROUND THE RIALTO BRIDGE
Shops, markets and picnic sites

Shops

Calle dei Speziali 18

🚤 Vaporetto Rialto

Open: Mon–Sat

If you walk across the Rialto Bridge towards the fish and vegetable markets, you come to Speziali. This only runs a short distance between two little *campos*, but has several good food and drink shops, which can sometimes be hidden by the souvenir stalls in the middle. The best is **Mascari** (*see below*) but there are many more which warrant a look.

Casa del Parmigiano 19

Casaria 240A

✆ 522 0825

🚤 Vaporetto Rialto

Open: Mon–Sat

A fantastic little food shop in the vegetable market specialising in cheeses and olive oils. There are dozens of oils available, either in individual bottles or as gift boxes containing several different varieties – a superb present for a foodloving friend. There's also fresh bread and cold meats, to make up a good picnic lunch.

Gros Point de Venise 20

Merceria San Salvador 5025

✆ 523 8175

🚤 Vaporetto Rialto

Open: Mon–Sat

All credit cards accepted

'Gros Point de Venise' is the term describing Venetian lace since the 17th century. This little shop can't compete in quality with those on the Piazza San Marco, but it has more affordable '*fatto a mano*'

(handmade) items, including tablecloths and plain or patterned napkins: how about a fun set featuring a gondola for those Italian-themed dinners?

Mascari 21

Calle dei Speziali 381

✆ 522 9762

🚤 Vaporetto Rialto

Open: Mon–Sat

No credit cards accepted

The enticing window displays here will make your mouth water. There are trays of coffee beans and various teas, such as camomile, or *karkade* tea from the Sudan. There are honeys in dozens of flavours, including eucalyptus and peach, a range of extra virgin olive oils and dried mushrooms, plus drinks including *vin santo* and port.

Rialto Bio Centre 6

Campo de la Beccarie 366

✆ 523 9515

🚤 Vaporetto Rialto

Open: Mon–Sat

No credit cards accepted

Venture a little beyond the fish and vegetable markets and you come to this organic and health food shop, where you can buy organically produced fruit, vegetables, cheeses, olive oils,

▲ Coffee beans for sale in Mascari

▲ Rialto Vegetable Market

pasta, honey, bread, soya and rice drinks, plus vitamins and health products too.

Ruga Vecchia San Giovanni 22

🚤 Vaporetto Rialto

Venice is very rich in good food shops and there is simply not room to single out anything other than the very best or the most distinctive. That still leaves hundreds of small shops, each one of them a treasure trove for the food and drink lover. You can find numerous such shops along the busy Ruga Vecchia San Giovanni, where you will find delicatessens, wine shops, ice-cream shops, a bakery and many others selling filled rolls and snacks to take away.

Markets

Rialto Fish Market 23

Campo Pescaria

🚤 Vaporetto Rialto

Open: Tue–Sat am

The fish market near the Rialto Bridge is a sight to see, just as much as any palace or museum, even if it is of no practical use to visitors other than the few people who self-cater while in the city. There are squid, crabs, shrimps, octopus, tuna, salmon, scallops, mussels, whelks and other fish of every size, some looking like monsters from your darkest nightmare.

Rialto Vegetable Market 24

Casaria

🚤 Vaporetto Rialto

Open: Mon–Sat am

Easily the best vegetable market in the city is next to the fish market but also opens on Monday when the fish market is closed. While the produce here is rather more familiar to most visitors, it is still a colourful sight well worth seeing. The best local fruit and vegetables include some from the lagoon island of Sant' Erasmo, which is said to be the best in the region, while other stalls sell organic produce.

Picnic sites

Rialto Bridge 25

🚤 Vaporetto Rialto

To suggest a picnic at the Rialto Bridge might at first appear to be madness, as it is almost permanently packed with visitors. However, if you go over the bridge from the southern (San Marco) side into the northern (San Polo) side, and turn left at the bottom, immediately under the bridge on your left there is a little recess with some stone walls to sit on. Here is one of the most wonderful views of the Grand Canal which you can enjoy while tucking into a snack, a cheaper alternative than dining at one of the several almost identical restaurants that line the canal here.

Feeding the family

The art of pleasing everyone

Venice is not the most obvious place to take young children on holiday, and it is noticeable how few families there are here, compared to other holiday destinations. Many visitors come from America and Japan, and tend to travel as couples or singles, as not many children are interested in the fine art and architecture, or the sheer unique beauty of the city.

Nevertheless, families do come here, and there are of course numerous Venetian and Italian families in the city, the babies constantly being bumped up and down the canal bridges in their pushchairs. If you decide to come here with children, you will have no trouble keeping them fed, whether their tastes are simple, sophisticated or some-where inbetween depending on their mood.

To begin with **breakfast**, this is usually a simple affair but will normally include the choice of hot chocolate to drink in addition to tea, coffee and orange juice. Rolls and croissants with jam and butter is the basic breakfast, with cold cheeses and meats available in slightly more up-market hotels, so nothing too controversial for fussy children to complain about, but cereals are less common.

During the day it will be difficult to avoid the regular demands for **ice cream**, as ice-cream shops (*gelaterie*) are everywhere. Even if you discourage children from eating too much ice cream at home, you ought to suspend the rules while in Venice as Italian ice cream is deli-cious and made with

natural ingredients. You can usually choose to have a cone or a tub, with a choice of one, two or three scoops, which can be of different flavours, but be warned that having more than one scoop on a cone can be tricky for a child to cope with, so stick to one scoop at a time if you want to avoid the tears that accompany spilled ice cream. Most places have a choice of at least a dozen flavours, including such delights as tiramisu, mint, *panna cotta* and chocolate.

At **lunchtime** there are plenty of informal eating places around, with pizza on most menus, and if you are in any doubt then the simplest thing is to check your map and head for a large *campo*, as most of them have at least one restaurant with outdoor seating, or a café serving simple snacks. If you have to have a simple dish, many places offer pizzas, steaks, chicken, chips, lasagne and other options which most children like, unless you happen to have a child who relishes the thought of squid cooked in its own ink! Don't be afraid to ask for something that's not on the menu, such as a bowl of plain spaghetti or pasta.

Alternatively, there are plenty of **fast-food** places around Venice, most of them concentrated in the central area between Piazza San Marco and the Rialto Bridge. Here you'll find **McDonald's**, **Burger King** and several Italian equivalents, though these will often also offer a slice of pizza to take away too. McDonald's seems to have sponsored at least half the litterbins in the city, so if you need to know how far it is to the nearest Big Mac, take a look at a litterbin.

Don't automatically only look for the places you would normally seek out at home. In Venice the categories merge even more than they do in the rest of Italy, and places described as *bacari* or *osteria*, which are most easily described as bars, frequently also sell filled rolls, sandwiches or pizza slices which children (and adults) will be perfectly happy to munch on in the street during the day, or take to one of the recommended picnic spots.

In the **evening** you will find that most Venetian places – as in the rest of Italy – are very child-friendly, and only a handful of the more expensive places, where you probably wouldn't want to take a child anyway, might look a bit askance at the arrival of very young children. The majority of eating places will offer children's portions, even if they are not actually listed on the menu, and will charge you a scaled-down version of the cost. Don't forget that the waiters and waitresses probably have children or grandchildren of their own, and know what it's like.

> **McDonald's seems to have sponsored at least half the litterbins in the city, so if you need to know how far it is to the nearest Big Mac, take a look at a litterbin.**

Castello

The Castello district to the east of the city centre is a real contrast. At one end it merges into the busy visitor-filled streets of San Marco, and up towards the Rialto Bridge, yet its backstreets contain many gems of places for eating and drinking, and crowds thin out the further east you walk.

CASTELLO
Restaurants

Da Bruno ❶

Calle del Paradiso 5731

✆ 522 1480

🚤 Vaporetto Rialto

Open: Wed–Mon lunch and dinner, closed one week in Jan

Reservations unnecessary

All credit cards accepted

Venetian

€

Unexceptional looking, outside and inside, the food here belies the décor, with excellent seasonal game dishes a speciality, and other treats such as smoked eel, *gnocchi* with gorgonzola or just a cheap but tasty pizza.

Corte Sconta ❷

Calle del Pestrin 3886

✆ 522 7024

🚤 Vaporetto Arsenale

Open: Tue–Sat lunch and dinner, closed for four weeks in Jan/Feb and four weeks in July/Aug

Reservations recommended

All credit cards accepted

Seafood

€€

Hard to find but worth the effort, this unpretentious and sprawling fish restaurant is always lively. Listen closely as the menu is recited for you, and go for whatever is fresh that day, simply grilled.

Al Covo ❸

Campiello della Pescaria 3968

✆ 522 3812

🚤 Vaporetto Arsenale

Open: Fri–Tue lunch and dinner

Reservations recommended

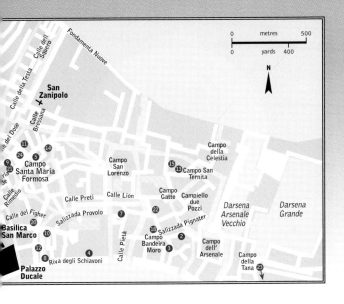

CORTE SCONTA

No credit cards accepted

Seafood

€€

This intimate little restaurant is one of the best places in Venice, serving imaginative dishes such as *gnocchetta* with red mullet ragout or grilled calamari with monkfish, which taste as good as they look.

Do Leoni 4

Londra Palace Hotel, Riva degli Schiavoni 4171

✆ 520 0533

🚤 Vaporetto San Zaccaria

Open: daily lunch and dinner

Reservations recommended

All credit cards accepted

International

€€€

Sidewalk terrace plus an elegant indoor room in this hotel restaurant which caters for visitors, locals and guests alike. The informal lunch and candlelit dinner features inventive dishes such as baked salmon in a champagne sauce.

Al Mascaron 5

Calle Lunga Santa Maria Formosa 5223

✆ 522 5995

🚤 Vaporetto Rialto

Open: Mon–Sat lunch and dinner, closed four weeks Dec/Jan

▲ Fresh anchovies at Al Covo

Reservations essential

No credit cards accepted

Venetian

💰💰

This wine bar's food has earned such a reputation that it is now a restaurant with three simply decorated rooms showing the seafood influence on the menu. Spaghetti with lobster is one of the chef's specialities.

Mondo Novo 6

Salizzada di San Lio 5409

✆ 520 0698

🚤 Vaporetto Rialto

Open: Tue–Sun lunch and dinner

Reservations recommended

All credit cards accepted

Seafood-Venetian

💰💰

Housed in a Renaissance building, this formal but relaxed restaurant concentrates on seafood with seasonal offerings such as sea bass fillet with artichokes or veal chop in spiced butter and mint sauce.

Da Remigio 7

Salizzada dei Greci 3416

✆ 523 0089

🚤 Vaporetto San Zaccaria

Open: Wed–Mon lunch, Wed–Sun dinner

Reservations recommended

All credit cards accepted

Venetian

💰💰

The Remigio may look no different from other places in this busy dining area, but the food is way ahead. A wide choice of fresh fish is usually available, along with a delicious fish risotto.

Ristorante Terrazza 8

4th Floor, Danieli Hotel, Riva degli Schiavoni 4196

✆ 522 6480

🚤 Vaporetto San Zaccaria

Open: daily lunch and dinner

Reservations recommended

All credit cards accepted

Seafood-Venetian

💰💰💰

The fourth-floor terrace restaurant offers diners one of the best views in the city. The food is immaculately prepared and presented, with dishes such as pan-fried John Dory and scampi tails with fresh tomato and capers.

Alle Testiere 9

Calla del Mondo Novo 5801

✆ 522 7220

🚤 Vaporetto Rialto

Open: Mon–Sat lunch and dinner

Reservations essential

All credit cards accepted

Seafood-Venetian

💶💶

A tiny and simple trattoria that is immensely popular, with two evening servings at 1900 and 2100. The creatively prepared dishes include such treats as *gnochetti* with *cala-*

maretti, or fillet of St Peter's fish with fresh vegetables.

Trattoria Alla Rivetta ⑩

Ponte San Provolo, Campo San Filippo 4625

✆ 528 7302

🚤 Vaporetto San Zaccaria

Open: Tue–Sun lunch and dinner, closed four weeks in July/Aug

Reservations recommended

💳 💳 American Express

Seafood

💶

Diners in this exceptional seafood place are packed in like, appropriately, sardines. The décor is simple and the noise level high, and you have to join the queue if you haven't booked. Try *gnocchi* stuffed with spidercrab, or mixed grilled fish.

CASTELLO
Bars, cafés and pubs

Bar all' Orologio ⑪

Campo Santa Maria
Formosa 6130

✆ 523 0515

🚤 Vaporetto Rialto

Open: Mon–Sat day and
evening

No credit cards accepted

Great place for watching the goings-on in the *campo*, though a little on the pricey side. The usual beers, wines, teas and coffees are supplemented by simple snacks such as filled rolls, pizza slices or toasted sandwiches.

Birreria Forst ⑫

Calle delle Rasse 4540

✆ 523 0557

🚤 Vaporetto San Zaccaria

Open: daily till late

No credit cards accepted

A cosy little bar-café not far from San Marco but a world away in feeling. It serves simple snacks such as panini, pizza and toast, as well as a range of wines from the barrel, liqueurs, beers, soft drinks and coffee, too.

Ae do Marie ⑬

Calle del'Olio 3129

✆ 523 5685

🚤 Vaporetto Celestia

Open: Mon–Sat all day

No credit cards accepted

This little place is about as backstreet as you can get, and if you venture here you'll probably be the only non-local present. Food and wine are both simple and cheap (as indeed is the décor), and you could spend an entire evening here for less than the price of a pizza near San Marco.

Alla Mascareta ⑭

Calle Santa Maria Formosa
5138

✆ 523 0744

🚤 Vaporetto Rialto

Open: Mon–Sat evenings
only

No credit cards accepted

This bright-looking and busy wine bar has the same owners as the nearby **Al Mascaron** restaurant (*see page 39*), but here the emphasis is firmly on the wine with a wide list available, from the Veneto and beyond. There are simple snacks, but people come here mainly to drink and to talk, mingling with the background piano

INSALATA FRESCA 4400
PROSCIUTTO E MELONE 9500
ROAST-BEEF ALL'INGLESE 5
PATATE IN PADELLA 3800
BISTECCA DI ROAST-BEEF 8

music, and it's the perfect place to repair to before or after a meal at the Mascaron ... or before and after.

Morion

Calle del Morion 2951

✆ 520 5163

🚤 Vaporetto Ospedale Civile

Open: daily till late

No credit cards accepted

A venue for the more adventurous, being a cross between a social centre, a bar, a café and a music venue, serving simple sandwiches and snacks, wine and beer, and with regular rock, blues, jazz and reggae concerts, way out in the backstreets of Castello.

L'Olandese Volante 🔵

Campo San Lio 5658

✆ 528 9349

🚤 Vaporetto Rialto

Open: Mon–Sat till late

All credit cards accepted

You can't miss 'The Flying Dutchman',

whose tables fill the *campo* and are usually filled with diners at lunchtime and in the evening. You could easily miss the fact that inside is a great bar, a cool dark contrast to the square and reminiscent of both British pubs and Dutch 'brown bars'. Here you can get Murphy's, Double Diamond, Long Life and other beers, both draught and bottled, and enjoy the relaxed atmosphere too.

Osteria al Portego 🔵

Calle Malvasia 6015

✆ 522 9038

🚤 Vaporetto Rialto

Open: Mon–Fri till 2200 and Sat till 1500

No credit cards accepted

This backstreet *bacari* has a good choice of wines including Sauvignon, Cabernet, Merlot, Chardonnay and the local fizzy white wine, Prosecco. The tiny

bar has several small barrels, and if you're lucky you might be able to grab one of the handful of tables and tuck into the better-than-average food, from bar nibbles to full meals such as seafood risotto.

Alla Rampa 🔵

Salizzada Sant' Antonio 3607

✆ 523 0024

🚤 Vaporetto San Zaccaria

Open: Mon–Sat all day till 2030

No credit cards accepted

A simple little corner café-bar with barely room for one table inside, and a barrel to rest your drinks on. It exudes a friendly neighbourhood feel, if you can find the neighbourhood, and the few visitors who venture here are welcomed warmly. The Rampa also serves basic snacks such as panini or toast to have with your beer or glass of wine.

CASTELLO
Shops, markets and picnic sites

Shops

Bottiglieria Colonna ⑲

Calle della Fava 5595

☏ 528 5137

🚤 Vaporetto Rialto

Open: Mon–Sat am and early evening

No credit cards accepted

This excellent wine shop is easily missed on a dark and narrow side street just off the Campo San Lio. Take a look, as the extensive selection includes many local wines, as well as a good stock of other regional wines from throughout Italy. There are brandies such as Remy Martin, liqueurs such as Calvados, and a range of olive oils too. There are gift boxes, and the shop will ship overseas if you spend

madly ... though, strangely, they don't take credit cards.

Pauly and Co ⑳

Ponte dei Consorzi, Calle Large San Marco 4391A

☏ 520 9899

🚤 Vaporetto San Zaccaria

Open: daily in summer, Mon–Sat am and pm in winter

All credit cards accepted

This grand glass emporium has museum-like displays and a vast stock of Murano glass, but don't be discouraged by the classy atmosphere as the staff are friendly and prices are reasonable, a notch cheaper than on nearby Piazza San Marco.

Ratti ㉑

Calle delle Bande 5825

☏ 520 0622

🚤 Vaporetto San Zaccaria

Open: Mon–Fri am and pm, Sat am

💳 💳 American Express

The window displays of this huge shop are not exactly inspiring and you might be forgiven for just passing by. It sells every household appliance and electrical item you can think of, but in among them is a terrific stock of kitchenware, so if you want a good-quality and inexpensive Italian coffeepot or garlic crusher, or some handy gadget you can't find at home, take a look in here.

Vino e ... Vini ㉒

Fondamenta dei Furlani 3301

☏ 521 0184

🚤 Vaporetto San Zaccaria

Open: Mon–Sat am and early evening

All credit cards accepted

A smart wine shop with a pleasant canal-side setting, whose narrow frontage conceals a large interior. If you want to try Venetian wines then there is a good selection, but you can also choose from stock from the rest of Italy and indeed the rest of the world, from Moët et Chandon to Californian Zinfandel. But if you just want a humble Italian

Lambrusco, you can get that too.

Markets

Via Guiseppe Garibaldi Market 23

🚤 Vaporetto Arsenale

Open: Mon–Sat am

Towards the eastern end of Castello is one of Venice's great secrets ... or at least secret from most of its visitors. Via Garibaldi is a long and wide street that's lined with unpretentious and inexpensive little cafés and restaurants, as well as numerous food shops and, in the mornings, a decent number of market stalls too. Here are delis and bakers, fruit and veg stalls, fish stalls, a floating grocery at the northern end, and shops selling pasta including tagliatelle already flavoured with squid ink and curry-flavoured fettucine.

▲ Via Giuseppe Garibaldi Market

Picnic sites

Campiello di Angelo 22

Junction of V. Giuseppe Garibaldi and Vle Giuseppe Garibaldi

🚤 Vaporetto Arsenale

Just off the Via Garibaldi shops and stalls is this little square with some shade and a few benches to sit on, the perfect place to take a picnic put together from the market traders or in the local delis.

Campo Bandiera Moro 7

🚤 Vaporetto Arsenale

Just back from the waterfront is this tiny square where you can immediately switch from being a tourist to feeling like a local. The handful of benches often have old men sitting on them, chatting away just like in the backstreet of any small Mediterranean town. The high buildings surrounding the little square provide shade, and a few old wells add character ... all you need to do is put together a picnic lunch, perhaps from the great food shops along the

nearby Via Garibaldi (*see above*).

Campo Santa Maria Formosa 24

🚤 Vaporetto Rialto

This lovely large square is great for relaxing in the sunshine, with several benches, some shade from the tall buildings, and a constant passing parade of tourists and locals to keep you entertained. There are a few cafés if you want to buy a cup of coffee or a cold drink, and in the mornings a handful of fruit and veg stalls, though hardly enough to warrant the description of a market.

Late-night wining and dining

Restrained revelry

For several very good reasons, Venice has never been known as a late-night city. The place itself is so small and compact that the noise from any late-night revelry would disturb thousands of people, so there are noise restrictions to prevent this. In addition, space is so tight that it would be hard to find a suitable property in which to house cavernous discos, even if they could be sound-proofed. Then there are the visitors, who are mostly middle-aged to elderly, and for whom a late-night revel is a coffee in Piazza San Marco while listening to one of the mini-orchestras playing *Strangers in the Night*.

In fact, if your idea of late-night revelry *is* something sedate like that, then the **Piazza San Marco** will provide it in abundance. The many cafés stay open till midnight on most nights, and if you arrive in Venice late at night there can be no more magical experience than walking into the illuminated piazza to the sound of orchestral music, then gazing at the basilica and surrounding buildings while sipping on a glass of champagne ... or merely a cup of coffee. If you are in need of something to eat, some of the cafés do serve snacks, but not all of them, so check first.

If you are in need of a meal rather than a snack, then you need to be aware that the majority of restaurants do close comparatively early. One place that is central and open every day until 0100 (though the kitchen will close at about 0030) is the excellent **Le Bistrot de Venise** (*see page*

18) just a couple of minutes from the Piazza San Marco. It often has live events such as poetry readings or small concerts, or you can simply sit at one of the outdoor tables and tuck into a plate of pasta or one of their wacky astrological pizzas. It's a place of great character and atmosphere, and late diners may find themselves drawn back time and again.

If you want a choice of late-night venues, then there are two places to head for. One is the **Campo Santa Margherita** in Dorsoduro, which has become a magnet for anyone who considers midnight too early to go to bed. There are several cafés and bars here, which not only stay open all day, they stay open until about 0200 almost every night of the week.

The café-bar **Margaret DuChamp** (see page 83) is open every night, and is a very fashionable hangout for young Venetians. In fact you'll be lucky to find a seat at one of the outdoor tables – and there are lots of them – as it does get very busy. Outside you'll hear the buzz of conversation and friendly argument, and inside in the alcoves and along the bar is even more noise, from more talk augmented by piped music.

If Margaret DuChamp is a little too pretentious for you, then just stroll around the *campo* where there are several other late-night options, or on a warm evening simply sit on the benches and take in the scene.

The other good late-night place is over in Cannaregio, along the Fondamenta della Misericordia, where there's late-night eating and drinking in several places. For food try the **Iguana** (*no 2515; ✆ 716 722; ⚓ vaporetto Madonna dell'Orto; open: Tue–Sun 0800–1500, 1800–0100; reservations unnecessary; all credit cards accepted; ❶*). This Mexican café-bar gets lively early evening during the happy hour (which lasts 90 minutes from 1800) and again late at night when other places close down, but here you can still tuck into a taco or a tequila.

> **It doesn't look much from the outside, but inside you'll find tables to eat at, or drink at, and you might get anything from live reggae to chamber music.**

Further along the Fondamenta is **Paradiso Perduto** (*no 2540; ✆ 720 581; ⚓ vaporetto San Marcuola; open: Thu–Mon evenings only till 0200 and Sun lunch; reservations unnecessary; no credit cards accepted; ❶❶*). This mix of a bar, restaurant (till 2300) and music venue was one of the first in the city to stay open late, and so has its long-time fans. It doesn't look much from the outside, but inside you'll find tables to eat at, or drink at, and you might get anything from live reggae to chamber music.

There may not be many late-night places in Venice, but the ones that there are certainly have character and variety.

Cannaregio

Wedged between the Grand Canal on the south and the lagoon to the north, the most northern sestiere of Venice also stretches from the modern train station in the west to the borders of the Rialto Bridge and San Marco district in the east. Within those boundaries are modern shopping streets and some of the oldest quarters in Venice, and the restaurants and bars reflect this diversity.

CANNAREGIO
Restaurants

Antica Mola ❶

Fondamenta degli Ormesini 2800

✆ 717 492

🚤 Vaporetto San Marcuola

Open: daily lunch and dinner

Reservations unnecessary

All credit cards accepted

Venetian

❸

This place is in a lovely setting by a wide canal, though there's a delightful rear garden too. The menu in this 150-year-old trattoria is basic, but the food is good, including squid with polenta, spaghetti with clams and pepper steak.

Antiche Cantine Ardenghi ❷

Calle della Testa 6370

✆ 523 7691

🚤 Vaporetto Fondamenta Nuove

Open: Mon–Sat dinner

Reservations essential

No credit cards accepted

Venetian

❸❸

This one-time *osteria* is now only open for evening meals, and its tiny and cosy interior means that booking is essential. The fixed menu includes four courses of Venetian dishes such as stewed eel with polenta, plus limitless drinks.

Bentigodi ❸

Calleselle 1423

✆ 716 269

🚤 Vaporetto San Marcuola

Open: Mon–Sat lunch and dinner

Reservations recommended

No credit cards accepted

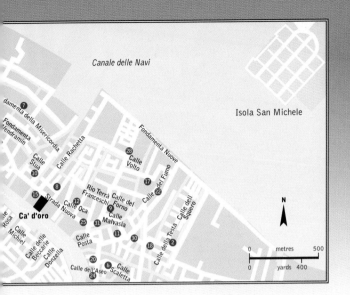

Canale delle Navi

Isola San Michele

Venetian

 €

A fabulous *osteria* with white walls and wooden ceilings, appealing to elderly locals having a drink and appreciative diners alike. The inventive menu depends on the market, but may include spaghetti with scallops and artichokes, or stuffed sardines.

Gam-Gam

Sotto Portego del Ghetto Veccio 1122

✆ 715 284

🚉 Vaporetto Guglie

Open: Sun–Thu lunch and dinner plus Fri lunch, Nov–Mar open Sat dinner

Reservations recommended

All credit cards accepted

Kosher-International

€€

With several canalside tables, and on the edge of the world's first ghetto, this smart and friendly place covers Jewish cuisine from several areas. Try *taglioni* with salmon, fish fillet with *haraimi* sauce or baked sea bass.

Il Melograno

Calle Riello 458B

✆ 524 2553

🚉 Vaporetto Guglie

Open: Tue–Sat lunch and dinner and Sun lunch

Reservations recommended

All credit cards accepted

International-Venetian

€€

The bright and cheerful 'Pomegranate' is unusual in presenting a truly international menu, with dishes such as baked blackened chicken from France, plus Venetian specialities like John Dory with a vegetable sauce.

Il Milion

Corte Prima al Milion 5841

✆ 522 9302

🚉 Vaporetto Rialto

Open: Thu–Tue lunch and dinner, closed Aug

Reservations recommended

No credit cards accepted

Venetian

€

▲ Antica Mola

This 300-year-old trattoria is one of the oldest in Venice, in a house that once belonged to Marco Polo's family. Dine on Venetian recipes such as calves' liver Venetian-style or spaghetti with clams.

Sahara ⑦

Fondamenta della
Misericordia 2519

☎ 721 077

🚇 Vaporetto Madonna dell'Orto

Open: Tue–Sun lunch and dinner

Reservations unnecessary

No credit cards accepted

Syrian-Middle Eastern

❸

Syrian cooking in a cosy café-like place, with no bar but down-to-earth prices for typical Arabic dishes such as *falafel*, kebabs, couscous and *tabouleh*. A lively and friendly atmosphere pervades, especially on weekend evenings when there's a belly-dancer.

Trattoria Ca' d'Oro **❽**

Ramo Ca' d'Oro 3912

✆ 528 5324

🚤 Vaporetto Ca' d'Oro

Open: Fri–Wed lunch and dinner, closed Sun lunch and in Aug

Reservations unnecessary

No credit cards accepted

Venetian

❸

You can book the tables, or take pot luck standing at the bar with a glass of wine (there's a good, wide range) and one of the tasty *cichetti*, such as *polpete* (spicy meatballs), fried calamari, cheeses and hams.

A La Vecia Cavana **❾**

Rio Terra del SS. Apostoli 4624

✆ 528 7106

🚤 Vaporetto Ca' d'Oro

Open: Fri–Wed lunch and dinner

Reservations recommended

All credit cards accepted

Seafood-Venetian

❸❸

Not too far from the Rialto Bridge, if you don't mind a backstreet adventure, this large and sophisticated place with its brickwork and

tile floors has an excellent seafood menu, including fish soup and three different seafood risottos.

Vini da Gigio **❿**

Fondamenta San Felice 3628A

✆ 528 5140

🚤 Vaporetto Ca' d'Oro

Open: Tue–Sun lunch and dinner

Reservations essential

All credit cards accepted

Venetian

❸❸

One of the city's best-value places for good food, the white walls and beamed ceiling of the Vini da Gigio reflect comfortable tradition. The seafood is excellent, but so is the game, when in season, such as duck breast in red wine.

▲ Bentigodi

CANNAREGIO
Bars, cafés and pubs

Boldrin ⓫

Salizzada San Chianciano 5550

✆ 523 7859

🚦 Vaporetto Sant' Angelo

Open: Mon–Sat 0900–2100

No credit cards accepted

This is a smart but easy-going kind of place that is part snack-bar, part wine-bar, with one wall lined completely with bottles. The bar-counter at the front dishes up the snacks and drinks and a blackboard tells you the day's specials, which might include lasagne or spaghetti with fish.

Alla Bomba ⓬

Call dell'Oca 4297

✆ 523 7452

🚦 Vaporetto Ca' d'Oro

Open: Thu–Tue lunch and dinner

No credit cards accepted

What looks at first to be a cosy little bar turns out to have a large dining room, where everyone sits side by side, or you can snack at the bar on the dishes laid out under the counter. Just off the busy Strada Nova, this is a great neighbourhood *bacaro*.

Cantina Vecia Carbonera ⓭

Ponte Sant' Antonio 2392

✆ 710 376

🚦 Vaporetto San Marcuola

Open: Tue–Sun from 1700

No credit cards accepted

Open till late, this may look like an ancient bar but it is in fact fairly new, but with traditional décor. It appeals more to young drinkers, especially at the weekends when it stays open till 0200 with live music on a Sunday.

Enoteca do Colonne ⓮

Rio Tera del Cristo 1814C

✆ 524 0453

🚦 Vaporetto San Marcuola

Open: Wed–Mon am, lunch and evenings

No credit cards accepted

A boisterous bar with a few tables outside attracting the few passing tourists, and shoppers, and inside the men of the neighbourhood gather to drink, argue and eat the tempting-looking bar snacks. There's a wide choice of wines available by the glass.

Fiddler's Elbow ⓯

Corte dei Pali 3487

✆ 523 9930

🚦 Vaporetto Ca' d'Oro

Open: daily from 1700

No credit cards accepted

The Italians and the Irish both like a good time, and this boisterous bar appeals to young Venetians, ex-pats and visitors alike. Guinness is on draught, and there are numerous other beers, along with a wide range of Irish whiskeys. There's live Celtic music on Wednesday and Sunday nights in the summer.

Osteria alla Fontana ⓰

Fondamenta Cannaregio 1102

✆ 715 077

🚦 Vaporetto Guglie

Open: Mon–Sat am, lunch and evenings, closed Wed pm and Aug

No credit cards accepted

This fantastic bar right by a canal is a touch of history, with cheeses and hams on the counter, to be weighed out for you if you fancy a snack, and wine sloshed into your glass from huge bottles. A speciality is *grissini*, which is Parma ham twisted round a bread stick. Very moreish.

Osteria alla Frasca ⓱

Corte della Carita 5176

✆ 528 5433

🚦 Vaporetto Fondamenta Nuove

Open: Fri–Wed am, lunch
and evenings, closed one
week in Aug and two weeks
in Jan

No credit cards accepted

There are tables outside
the Frasca in a beautiful
quiet courtyard, but
none inside where you
stand at the bar and
drink or sample the
snacks such as ham and
melon or squid
Venetian-style. There's
occasional live music
too.

Osteria da Alberto

Calle Larga Giacinto Gallina
5401

✆ 523 8153

🚉 Vaporetto Fondamenta
Nuove

Open: Mon–Sat am and
evenings

No credit cards accepted

Squeezed between two
bridges, with a canal
running by the side, the
Alberto is a simple little
place with a bar at the
front and tables beyond,
which you can book if
you want a meal rather
than just a drink. The
food is better elsewhere
but it's a popular neigh-
bourhood spot.

De Rossi ⑲

Rio Tera San Leonardo
1409

✆ 718 245

🚉 Vaporetto Ca' d'Oro

Open: Mon–Sat all day

VISA

Lively bar on a happen-
ing street, the Rossi also
serves as a café, a take-
away food shop, a wine
shop and a general

---

meeting place for local
people enjoying the
unpretentious atmos-
phere and the cheap
prices.

Tiziano Bar ⑳

Salizzada San Giovanni
Cristotomo 5747

✆ 523 5544

🚉 Vaporetto Rialto

Open: Sun–Fri till 2230

No credit cards accepted

A very lively local
snack bar where the
clatter of crockery and
glasses mixes with the
chatter of locals enjoy-
ing a drink. It looks a
little plastic at first,
with a fast-food service,
as well as bar snacks
and takeaways (it sells
pizza by the metre), but
it's still a good-
humoured place, great
for a cheap eat or drink.

CANNAREGIO
Shops, markets and picnic sites

Shops

Cibele ㉑

Campiello Anconetta 1823

✆ 524 2113

● Vaporetto San Marcuola

Open: Tue–Sat am and evening, and Mon evening

A bright little health-food store on a busy *campo*, with pastas, olive oil, biscuits, rice cakes, honey and other organic or just plain healthy products, along with vitamins, medicines, cosmetics and a range of herbal teas.

Constantini ㉒

Calle del Fumo 5311

✆ 522 2265

● Vaporetto Fondamenta Nuove

Open: Mon–Sat, closed lunchtime

All credit cards accepted

An exceptional glassware shop exhibiting the work of the owner, Vittorio Constantini, who is renowned for the quality of his creations. There are many purely decorative items, but also table lamps, dishes and wineglasses that would enhance any table.

Giovanni Volpe ㉓

Ghetto Vecchio 1143

✆ 715 178

● Vaporetto Guglie

Open: Mon–Sat, closed Wed pm

No credit cards accepted

An excellent bakery in the Jewish ghetto, producing kosher bread, but from a baker who isn't Jewish himself – he learned his trade from a Jewish baker. You'll find mouth-watering displays of pastries and biscuits, as well as loaves and rolls, and there is also a grocery section.

Rizzo ㉔

Calle San Giovanni Crisostomo 5778

✆ 522 2824

● Vaporetto Rialto

Open: Mon–Sat, closed lunchtime and Wed pm

No credit cards accepted

▲ Rio Terra San Leonardo Market

An exceptional food shop, even by Venetian standards. One wall is filled with pre-packed pastas, in every colour and flavour imaginable ... and some shapes better kept away from the children. Local products include olive oil and truffle drops, and international items include curry sauces, muffin mix, fava beans, guacamole seasoning, HP salsa and *teriyaki*. An Aladdin's cave for the international cook.

Strada Nova ㉕

🚤 Vaporetto Ca' d'Oro

This busy shopping street is great for food shops, including patisseries and delicatessens, and there are plenty of bars and cafés selling snacks, a McDonald's for the youngsters, and just a few yards away down some of the side streets are some wonderful bars and restaurants (*see map on page 49*).

Vinaria Nave de Oro ㉖

Salizzada San Leonardo 1370

✆ 719 695

🚤 Vaporetto Guglie

Open: Tue–Sat am and evening, and Mon evening

No credit cards accepted

A tiny wine shop with a barrel outside and a long thin counter inside, with room for no more than half a dozen customers ... and usually

full. It will fill your bottle for you from any of several barrels behind the counter, and along the opposite wall is a limited range of bottled wines for sale too.

Markets

Rio Terra San Leonardo Market ㉗

🚤 Vaporetto Guglie

Open: Mon–Sat am

A busy market, and while none in Venice compares to the Rialto, this is still one of the best of the rest. There are a few fish stalls but mainly you'll find fruit and vegetables, with colourful displays of apples, oranges, melons, cherries, courgettes, vivid tomatoes and whatever else is in season.

Picnic sites

Campo dei Gesuiti ㉘

🚤 Vaporetto Fondamenta Nuove

Some benches here in this peaceful square have small tables and shade from an awning, while there is more shade elsewhere from trees and the high buildings that surround the *campo*. There's also a drinking fountain and a canal nearby on one side with a distant view of the lagoon at the end

of the street, plus a handy public toilet too.

Campo di Ghetto Nuovo ㉙

🚤 Vaporetto Guglie

Not only a peaceful place for a picnic but historic, too, in the heart of the Jewish ghetto. Venice is where the ghetto was born, from the Venetian dialect word *getar*, meaning to throw or to cast away. This wide *campo* has some seating but not a lot of shade, so in summer it is best visited early or late in the day when the tall buildings provide some protection from the sun.

Campo Santa Maria Nova ㉚

🚤 Vaporetto Rialto

With bright red benches under some trees, a corner café, a church in the centre, some shops and nearby some excellent delicatessens, Campo Santa Maria Nova makes a good spot to sit down and have a snack.

Campo SS Apostoli ㉛

🚤 Vaporetto Ca' d'Oro

Benches under the shade of trees, an old well, a canalside setting, a kiosk, a café, a few shops ... the perfect picnic place.

Eating on the islands

More to life than glass!

The smaller lagoon islands not only provide a good day out for the visitor to Venice, they also include a range of good eating places. A trip planned around a leisurely lunch at one of these is a welcome break from the busy city, and shows a side of Venetian life that many visitors miss.

Perhaps the most indulgent day out would be to go to dine in what is one of the finest restaurants, the **Cipriani** on **Giudecca** (*Giudecca 10; ✆ 520 7744; open: daily lunch and dinner, closed Nov–Mar; reservations essential; all credit cards accepted;* ❶❷❸). The Hotel Cipriani has its own private boat which leaves from San Marco and takes hotel and restaurant guests back and forth across the lagoon, a splendid way to start and end a meal. To sample the main hotel restaurant you would need to eat in the evening, when men must wear a jacket and tie, or during the day you could also book into the more casual **Club Cipp**, which looks back to San Marco, or the outdoor restaurant which overlooks the Olympic-size swimming pool. The food all comes from the same fine kitchen, and some of the menus overlap. Sea bass is one speciality, broiled and served with cherry tomatoes and oregano, or perhaps veal with asparagus in season. Leave room for the temptations of the dessert trolley, and prepare for a big bill.

▲ Island glass

Also on Giudecca is the cousin of Harry's Bar, and that's **Harry's Dolci** (*Giudecca 773; ℰ 522 4844;* 🔊 *vaporetto Sant' Eufemia; open: Wed-Mon lunch and dinner, closed Nov-Mar; reservations recommended; all credit cards accepted;* ❸❸❸). The terrace restaurant offers fabulous views of Venice, and prices almost as fabulous as at **Harry's Bar** itself (*see page 9*). The international menu is similar to Harry's, and might include risotto with clams and certainly carpaccio, but as the name suggests this is a place for the sweet-toothed, and the cakes, pastries and desserts are to die for.

The **Lido** is well-stocked with good eating places, with one well-named favourite being the **Favorita** (*V. Francesco Duodo 33; ℰ 526 1626;* 🔊 *vaporetto Lido di Venezia; open: Tue-Sun lunch and dinner; reservations recom-mended; all credit cards accepted;* ❸❸❸). With outdoor seating and two dining rooms, in the quieter San Nicolo district of the Lido, this is food worth making the journey for. Seafood is the spe-ciality, whether simply grilled fresh fish or incorporated into dishes such as pasta with baby squid and aubergine, or *gnocchi* cooked in a spidercrab sauce.

Vying with the Favorita as best place on the Lido, but slightly more affordable, is **Ristorante Belvedere** (*Pzle Santa Maria Elisabetta 4; ℰ 526 0115;* 🔊 *vaporetto Lido di Venezia; open: Tue-Sun lunch and dinner,* closed Nov-Feb; reservations recommended; all credit cards accepted; ❸❸). Right by the vaporetto stop, with outdoor seating and a bright and airy indoor dining room, this is popular with Venetians for weekend lunches, and while the menu isn't entirely fish-based, your best option is to go for the chef's speciality: sea bass.

... dishes such as pasta with baby squid and aubergine, or gnocchi cooked in a spidercrab sauce ...

Murano caters more for the tourists who come over to buy the famous glass at source, but a good place that's usually busy with locals is the **Antica Trattoria** (*Fondamenta Cavour (Riva Lunga) 10; ℰ 739 610;* 🔊 *vaporetto Murano Museo; open: daily for lunch; reservations unnecessary; all credit cards accepted;* ❸❸). There's an attractive rear garden which makes the perfect spot for a slow trawl through the simple menu, which has plenty of pasta options, fresh fish grilled, or Venetian dishes such as squid in its own ink served with fried polenta.

On **Burano** the busiest place is usually right on the main square, **Ai Pescatori** (*V. Baldassare Galuppi 371; ℰ 730 650;* 🔊 *ferry line 12 from Fondamenta Nuove; open: Thu-Tue lunch and dinner; reservations recommended; all credit cards accepted;* ❸❸). Unusually for the location, and the name of the restaurant, game dishes are a speciality, though their seafood risotto is highly recommended.

San Polo

San Polo has been the liveliest quarter of Venice since the 11th century when it became the centre for the city's markets, and even though these have been singled out in the Rialto Bridge chapter, there still remain many backstreets to explore with their food shops and lesser-known eating places.

Map area:
Stazione FS Santa Lucia · Fondamenta Santa Lucia · Fondamenta San Simeon Piccolo · Fondamenta Tolentini · Piazzale Roma · Calle Clero · Sali · San Pa · Fondamenta Gaffaro

---

SAN POLO
Restaurants

Antica Ostaria Ruga Rialto ❶

Calle del Sturion 692

✆ 521 1243

🚉 Vaporetto Rialto

Open: Tue–Sun lunch and dinner

Reservations not allowed

💳

Venetian

❸

The unassuming entrance leads into a busy and unusually smart *osteria* where you can dine at the bar or at tables in one of the three rooms. A typical day's menu might include spaghetti in squid ink, *sarde* (sardines) in *saor* (sweet-and-sour sauce) or a *cicchetti misti* (mixed plate of snacks).

Le Carampane ❷

Rio Terra de la Carampane 1911

✆ 524 0165

🚉 Vaporettb San Silvestro

Open: Tue–Sat and Sun lunch, closed Aug

Reservations recommended

All credit cards accepted

Venetian-Seafood

❻❻

Really hidden away in San Polo (the street doesn't even appear on some maps) but worth finding for the exuberant atmosphere and the superb fish. Ask for what's fresh that day, or go for the *fritto misto*, the mixed fried selection, and leave room for the homemade biscuits.

Da Fiore ❸

Calle del Scaleter 2202

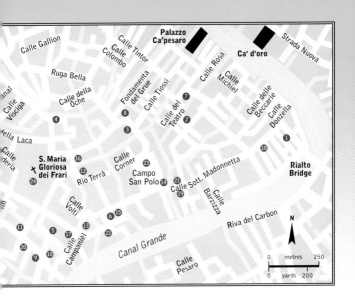

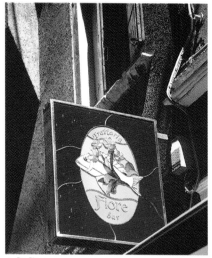

▲ Da Fiore

✆ 721 308

🚤 Vaporetto San Toma

Open: Tue–Sat lunch and dinner, closed three weeks in Aug and Christmas/New Year

Reservations essential

All credit cards accepted

Seafood

€€

Another backstreet place that's worth the effort of finding, for the warm welcome and the fresh fish, which could be the catch of the day simply grilled or something unusual the chef happened to see in the Rialto market. Sea bass with balsamic vinegar is also recommended.

Ganesh Ji ❹

Rio Marin 2426

✆ 719 804

🚤 Vaporetto Riva di Biaso

Open: Thu–Tue lunch and dinner

Reservations unnecessary

Indian

€

Chicken dishes are a speciality in this pleasant little Indian restaurant, with chicken *shaki*, chicken korma and chicken tikka all on the menu. So too is Kashmiri *rogan josh*, and they also offer a set menu for vegetarians.

Giardinetto ❺

Fondamenta del Forner 2910

✆ 522 4100

🚤 Vaporetto San Toma

Open: Tue–Sun lunch and dinner

Reservations unnecessary

All credit cards accepted

Venetian-Seafood

€€

A restaurant which also does pizzas in a wood-burning oven, an increasingly rare phenomenon in Venice. The place is relaxed and unpretentious and the menu ranges from staples such as squid in its own ink to risotto with scampi and vegetables. There's a garden dining area in summer.

Da Ignazio ❻

Calle dei Saoneri 2749

✆ 523 4852

🚤 Vaporetto San Toma

Open: Sun–Fri lunch and dinner

Reservations unnecessary

All credit cards accepted

Venetian

€€

A simple trattoria between Campo San Polo and Campo San Rocco, whose menu includes all the expected Venetian dishes such as calves' liver and squid with polenta, but there are some unusual seasonal offerings such as turbot with artichokes.

La Regina ❼

Calle della Regina 2331

✆ 524 1402

🚤 Vaporetto San Stae

Open: Tue–Sun lunch and dinner

Reservations recommended

All credit cards accepted

Italian-French

€€€

An up-market restaurant in the normally simple San Polo area, which takes the best local ingredients and adds a little flair to the usual recipes. A tasting menu allows you to sample the kitchen's best offerings.

Da Renato ⑧

Rio Tera Secondo 2245A

☏ 524 1922

🚤 Vaporetto San Stae

Open: Fri–Wed

Reservations unnecessary

No credit cards accepted

Venetian

€

If you're in the neighbourhood then call in at Renato's (the owner, who both cooks and waits on table) for a very special Venetian experience. You can't

fail to be charmed by the homely atmosphere and simple food, such as pasta and bean soup or a mixed fish fry.

Trattoria Ca' Foscari ⑨

Calle Foscari 3854

☏ 522 9216

🚤 Vaporetto San Toma

Open: daily lunch and dinner

Reservations unnecessary

All credit cards accepted

Venetian

€

A smart little trattoria with outdoor tables on a quiet street near the Foscari University. The menu includes simple but traditional Venetian fare such as spaghetti with cuttlefish cooked in its own ink, and tasty fried calamari.

Trattoria Dona Onesta ⑩

Calle della Madonna Onesta 3922

☏ 710 586

🚤 Vaporetto San Toma

Open: Mon–Sat lunch and dinner

Reservations unnecessary

All credit cards accepted

Venetian-Seafood

€€

An old-fashioned trattoria style and a traditional menu make for a cosy atmosphere in an elegant setting at the 'Honest Woman' (there are various suggestions as to how the place got its name). The predictable but tasty bill of fare includes spaghetti with squid, squid cooked in its own ink, and seafood risotto.

SAN POLO
Bars, cafés and pubs

Café Blue ⑪

Calle della Verona 3778

✆ 528 7998

🚊 Vaporetto San Toma

Open: Mon–Sat 0700–0200

No credit cards accepted

This youthful café-bar is popular with students from the nearby university as an all-day and late-night hangout and combines an almost aching trendiness with a charming amateurishness. There's coffee, beer, wine, a few snacks, board games if you get bored, a noticeboard, chat, an arty atmosphere and plenty of loud music which is sometimes live – a general feeling of a place where people hang out regularly.

Caffè dei Frari ⑫

Fondamenta dei Frari 2564

✆ 524 1877

🚊 Vaporetto San Toma

Open: daily

No credit cards accepted

A backstreet bar-café which appeals to students from the Foscari University nearby. It's a cosy place with cheap eats and drinks, and a constant music soundtrack. Not for everyone but if you like it then it could become addictive.

Ciak 1 ⑬

Campo San Toma 2807

✆ 528 5150

🚊 Vaporetto San Toma

Open: daily

💳 VISA

▲ Da Cico

Perfect on a sunny day with tables outside, but take a look inside if it's cooler as there are several divided booths along the wall if you want some privacy. Drinks and snacks are the usual fare, but the place does have character... and its characters.

Da Cico ⑭

Campo San Polo 1960

✆ None available

🚊 Vaporetto San Toma

Open: Mon–Sat

No credit cards accepted

Spotted by the outdoor tables with their generous green umbrellas for shade, this is a pleasant café-bar with a range of sandwiches to eat there or take away, desserts such as apple cakes or a Macedonia (fruit salad), and it also has its own delicious ice creams too.

Alla Patatina ⑮

Ponte San Polo 2741

✆ 523 7238

🚊 Vaporetto San Toma

Open: Mon–Fri lunch and dinner and Sat dinner

No credit cards accepted

A real old-fashioned *osteria* with barrels and bottles behind the bar and bar snacks under the counter, especially the potatoes that give the bar its name: try the roasted ones, or have a fully-fledged meal of pasta or risotto if you can grab a table. Otherwise enjoy the wine, the nibbles and the noisy amicable atmosphere.

Al Ponte 15

Ponte San Polo 2741

☎ 523 7238

🚤 Vaporetto San Toma

Open: Mon–Fri lunch and dinner, and Sat lunch, closed two weeks in Aug

A homely *bacaro* serving good food at cheap prices in a lovely canal-side location by a bridge. What more do you want? The perfect place to pass a lunchtime or evening, nibbling on snacks such as octopus, squid, ham and cheese.

San Stin 16

Campo San Stin 2248

☎ 524 1987

🚤 Vaporetto San Toma

Open: daily

No credit cards accepted

A typical Venetian café but on one of the smaller and quieter *campos* in this area, so it has a neighbourly feel and is a good place to head for if you want to relax over a cup of coffee or a glass of beer, or grab a pizza slice or a sandwich. It's only a minute from the much busier San Rocco.

San Toma 17

Campo San Toma 2864

☎ 523 8819

🚤 Vaporetto San Toma

Open: Wed–Mon lunch and dinner

All credit cards accepted

The cuisine in this café-restaurant is Venetian but the house speciality is a paella dish from Valencia, which needs to be ordered in advance, though you can also have simple pizzas and the usual Venetian offerings. There's a buzzing atmosphere and a cool rear garden as well as seating on the *campo* if you just fancy a drink.

Vivaldi 18

Calle della Madonetta 1457

☎ 523 8185

🚤 Vaporetto San Silvestro

Open: Mon–Sat lunch and dinner

No credit cards accepted

A simple *osteria* if you want to snack and drink rather than have a sit-down meal ... though there are plenty of tables available too. Try the pumpkin risotto, in season, or a mixed plate of the extraordinarily good bar snacks.

SAN POLO
Shops, markets and picnic sites

Shops

Aliani Gastronomia 19

Ruga Vecchia San Giovanni 655

☎ 522 4913

Ⓢ Vaporetto Rialto

Open: Mon–Sat, closed Mon and Wed pm

No credit cards accepted

A beautiful-looking up-market delicatessen/shop, which has the best of Italy's produce, ranging from hams and cheeses through to preserved truffles, balsamic vinegar, honey, wines and the best-quality pasta. The counter also has some pre-prepared salads, ideal for a gourmet picnic lunch.

La Bottega di Cenerentola 20

Calle dei Saoneri 2721

☎ 523 2006

Ⓢ Vaporetto San Toma

Open: Mon–Sat

All credit cards accepted

One of the best lace shops in Venice, away from the Piazza San Marco, with just as good-quality goods but at slightly lower prices (some are antique pieces so the prices are correspondingly higher). The perfect place to find a handmade lace tablecloth or smaller items for the table.

Rizzardini 21

Campiello dei Meloni 1415

☎ 522 3835

Ⓢ Vaporetto San Silvestro

Open: Wed–Mon

No credit cards accepted

A pastry shop *par excellence*, which might make you think you're in Vienna. The beautifully made and presented cakes and pastries are a treat for the eyes, as indeed is the old shop. Try one of the small chocolate cakes or fresh fruit tarts.

Sabbie e Nebbie 22

Rio Terra di Nomboli

☎ 719 073

Ⓢ Vaporetto San Toma

▲ Foscari University

SABBIE e NEBBIE

di MariaTeresa Laghi
San Polo, 2768/a Tel.041.719073
30125 - VENEZIA -

Open: Mon–Sat am and
early evening

A ceramics shop whose
featured artist, Maria
Teresa Laghi, is heavily
influenced by the styles
of Japan and the Far
East. She produces
exquisite handmade
bowls, vases and dishes,
lovely little cane-
handled teapots, chop-
sticks and holders.
Some of the blue plates
with white swirling
lines emanating from
the centre (which look
far more subtle than
they sound) are avail-
able in several sizes to
form a gorgeous and
striking dinner service.
Directly across from this
shop is just the opposite
– a down-to-earth
hardware store with a
good range of kitchen
items including coffee
grinders and percola-
tors, pots, nutcrackers,
garlic crushers, kitchen
knives and cutlery.

Picnic sites

Campo San Polo ㉓
🚊 Vaporetto San Silvestro

This huge square has
numerous benches
placed underneath
clumps of trees to pro-
vide some shade, with
some benches with
tables under a canopy,
courtesy of the Venetian
authorities. It makes a
good place to sit, sur-
rounded as it is by old
buildings, including the
Palazzo Soranzo and the
**Palazzo Corner
Mocenigo**. If you don't
want to overdose on
culture you can simply
enjoy a good ice cream
from the café on the
square, **Da Cico** (see
page 62). There is a
handy public toilet too.

Campo San
Rocco ㉔
🚊 Vaporetto San Toma

Campo San Rocco is a
big area but not much is
left over for people as
the bulk is given over to
the **Church of San
Rocco**, which has sev-
eral **Tintoretto** paintings
inside. On a more prac-
tical level, it also pro-
vides lots of shade
outside during most of
the day, and you can
usually find some steps
to sit on to enjoy a pic-
nic. It's a busy area and
there are several good
ice-cream places in par-
ticular, as well as cafés.

Last-minute buys

If you have any
money left over, save
it for the **Marco Polo
Airport** where there is
an excellent deli-
catessen/wine shop:
Mangilli (✆ 541 6210;
open: daily 0800–
2030; all credit cards
accepted). It is situ-
ated before you go
through passport con-
trol and though the
selection of drink is
smaller than in the
duty-free shop, it is of
much better quality
and includes fine
wines from the
Veneto, and a range
of grappas in attrac-
tive bottles (see pages
76–7 for advice on
what to buy). You
could also spend your
last few lire on olive
oil, balsamic vinegar,
dried mushrooms or
tomatoes, sauces or a
final bag of pasta.

Wines of the Veneto

Bottles made to be opened

Venice and the region around it, the Veneto, is Italy's largest producer of DOC (*denominazione di origine controllata*) wines – the Italian equivalent of *appellation* controlled wines. As a result, there is no shortage of good local wines to try, including several names that will be familiar to wine drinkers such as Soave, Valpolicella and Bardolino, and many new ones to discover as well.

A wine you will certainly become familiar with is **Prosecco**. This is the region's principal sparkling wine, and is available everywhere from the humblest bar to the priciest restaurant. A worker is just as likely to drink a glass on his way home as is the wealthiest Venetian. It is a very refreshing light white wine, and is usually dry (*seco*), although there is also a medium-sweet version

too (*amabile*). There are also two degrees of fizziness. *Spumante* is the fully sparkling version, while *frizzante* is slightly less so. You don't usually need to worry about these terms as if you walk into any bar and ask for a Prosecco, you will be given a glass of the house version. You needn't fret too much about the cost, either, as unless you are drinking it in somewhere like **Harry's Bar** (*see page 9*), it is a mere fraction of the cost of champagne. A Prosecco is a delightful end to the day's work for the locals or the start of an evening out for visitors, though you can continue the treat and drink a bottle with your meal if you like. It is one of the local wines that is most consistent in its quality. It may lack the subtlety of champagne but it is rare to get a truly bad glass. You can also find a delicious rosé version,

and the very best Prosecco of all is known as **Cantizze**. Prosecco is also the basis of the Bellini, invented at Harry's Bar, and other variations which mix it with different fruit juices to make a delightful aperitif.

Soave is a very easy-drinking wine, which it needs to be as over 52 million litres are produced every year. Not all of it is of good quality, but makers whose Soaves can be recommended include Anselmi, Bertani, CS di Soave, Guerrieri-Rizzardi, Masi, Pieropan, Tedeschi and Zenato. Soave goes well with appetisers, pasta dishes, fish and seafood.

Valpolicella is the best-known red wine, and like Soave this can vary enormously in quality, the worst examples being harsh and almost undrinkable. Again, look for a reliable winemaker if you want to be sure to avoid one of the vinegar-like varieties. Try vineyards such as Alighieri, Bertani, Guerrieri-Rizzardi, Masi, Tedeschi and Zenato. Don't confuse Valpolicella with Ripasso Valpolicella, which is a stronger and richer version, well suited to strong meat dishes. There is also Recioto della Valpolicella, which is a strong but sweet red wine.

Of the more familiar grape varieties, ones which grow well in the Veneto include **Tocai** and **Sauvignon** in the whites, and **Cabernet Sauvignon** and **Merlot** in the reds, and if you are a fan of any of those grapes you should find some satisfying

> **A Prosecco is a delightful end to the day's work for the locals or the start of an evening out for visitors.**

wines, though perhaps not of world-beating class. Local producers tend to produce wines to drink, and to drink young, rather than to win medals.

The third of the well-known local varieties is **Bardolino**, a light, dry red that is a good accompaniment to all kinds of meat dishes except perhaps for the heaviest game. The recommended manufacturers include most of the same names listed above for both Soave and Valpolicella. These are the grapes which grow best in the area and which are popular both in Italy and overseas, so it is hardly surprising to find vineyards producing all three.

Some of the less familiar wines to watch out for on menus and in the wine shops include **Amarone**, which is a very strong dry red, perhaps best sampled by the glass first, if possible, as it is not to everyone's taste, with a slightly bitter finish to it. But if you do like it, try it with hearty meat and game dishes. **Breganze** is another lesser-known region, producing several kinds of wine that are on many Venetian wine lists. Almost all are fairly 'safe' wines, light whites and fruity reds, which should offend no one's palate.

Finally, if you just want a cheap and cheerful drink, almost all restaurants will offer a house white and red, available by the litre or half-litre, and which can usually be relied on to be good drinking table wines.

Santa Croce

Santa Croce is one of the smallest sestieres of Venice, and often gets swallowed up into San Polo in city guides. This is a shame, as although it lacks attractions as such, it has many narrow backstreets, with bars and restaurants waiting to be discovered by the more adventurous visitor.

SANTA CROCE
Restaurants

Antica Bessetta ❶

Calle della Savia 1395

✆ 721 687/524 0428

🚤 Vaporetto Riva di Biasio

Open: Thu–Mon lunch and dinner and Wed dinner

Reservations recommended

No credit cards accepted

Venetian

€€

Allow time to find this backstreet place, but make time to go there. This 18th-century restaurant is renowned for its good-quality cuisine and its relaxed but smart ambience. Try the spidercrab or their scampi and artichoke risotto.

Brodo di Giuggiole ❷

Fondamenta Minotto 158

✆ 524 2486

🚤 Vaporetto Piazzale Roma

Open: Tue–Sun lunch and dinner

Reservations recommended

All credit cards accepted

Venetian-Seafood

€€

There's both garden and indoor seating in this unpretentious restaurant which serves up some delicious and unusual seafood dishes, such as *tagliolini* with crab and courgettes, or tiny fried crabs. If you can't decide and have a good appetite, go for the sampler menu.

Da Crecola ❸

Campo del Piovan 1459

✆ 524 1496

🚤 Vaporetto Riva di Biasio

Open: Wed–Mon lunch and dinner

Reservations unnecessary

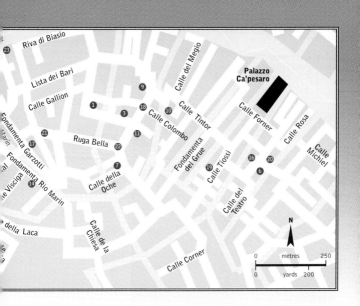

Riva di Biasio
Lista dei Bari
Calle Gallion
Fondamenta Garzotti
Fondamenta Marin
Ruga Bella
Fondamenta Rio Marin
Calle della Oche
della Laca
Calle de la Chiesa
Calle Corner
Calle del Megio
Calle Tintor
Palazzo Ca'pesaro
Calle Forner
Calle Rosa
Calle Michiel
Calle Colombo
Fondamenta del Grue
Calle Tiossi
Calle del Teatro

| | metres | 250 |
| 0 | yards | 200 |

▲ Al Ponte

If you want to eat near
the bus station, head for
this pizzeria/restaurant
with its white walls and
wooden beams. There
are classic pizzas such
as mushroom, tuna,
ham and cheese, four
seasons, and so on, but
try a speciality one,
such as the spiced pizza.

Al Nono Risorto ❻

Calle del Regina 2337

☎ 524 1169

🚤 Vaporetto San Stae

Open: Fri–Tue lunch and
dinner, and Thu dinner

Reservations unnecessary

No credit cards accepted

Italian

€

This lively place is
always packed with
young people. It has an
attractive garden area
with trees providing
shade, and as well as a
pizza menu, there are
Venetian dishes such as
squid in its own ink, and
a fixed-price menu too.

Ae Oche ❼

Calle del Tintos 1552

☎ 524 1161

🚤 Vaporetto San Stae

Open: Open daily
1200–2400, closed Mon in
winter

Reservations unnecessary

All credit cards accepted

Italian

€

All credit cards accepted

Italian

€

Some shaded seating
out on this lovely
campo and the Crecola's
menu is simple: inex-
pensive but reliable. The
long list of pasta dishes
is only exceeded by sev-
eral dozen pizzas, with
delights such as ricotta
and spinach on offer.

Dalle Zanze ❹

Fondamenta Tolentini 231

☎ 522 3555

🚤 Vaporetto Piazzale Roma

Open: Mon–Sat lunch and
dinner

Reservations essential

All credit cards accepted

Venetian-Seafood

€€

There's one small and
smart wood-beamed
dining room in this
long-established restau-
rant, where seafood is
the speciality. Try
linguini with crabmeat
or one of the imagina-
tive fish dishes such as
stargazer fish baked and
then marinated in
vinegar.

Al Gallo ❺

E. Corte Amai 197

☎ 520 5953

🚤 Vaporetto Piazzale Roma

The décor in this trattoria/pizzeria is so rustic it has been compared to a Western saloon. It's very relaxing and appeals to a slightly younger crowd. With 80 different pizzas to choose from, 16 salads and a full menu.

Papadopoli Restaurant

Hotel Sofitel, Pzle Roma

⌀ 710 400

🚤 Vaporetto Piazzale Roma

Open: daily lunch and dinner

Reservations recommended

All credit cards accepted

Venetian-International

€€€

This restaurant on the ground floor of the Sofitel Hotel has a sophisticated atmosphere and a creative menu. How about angler fish with wild mushrooms, perhaps accompanied by cream of potatoes with truffle oil?

Al Ponte 9

Ponte del Megio 1666

⌀ 719 777

🚤 Vaporetto San Stae

Open: Mon–Fri 0800–0100, Sat 0800–1500

Reservations recommended

No credit cards accepted

Venetian

€€

This place is in a wonderful location at the foot of a bridge, and has a great traditional trattoria atmosphere too, simple but excellent Venetian cuisine. Try

their Venetian liver, the fish fry, or any of the tasty pasta dishes.

Alla Zucca 10

Ponte del Megio 1762

⌀ 524 1570

🚤 Vaporetto San Stae

Open: Mon–Sat lunch and dinner

Reservations recommended

All credit cards accepted

Venetian

€

No one should visit Venice without dining at this kind of simple but atmospheric canalside trattoria, serving good, imaginative but inexpensive local food such as veal in a tuna sauce or peppers marinated in balsamic vinegar.

▲ Alla Zucca

SANTA CROCE
Bars, cafés and pubs

Capitan Uncino

Campo San Giacomo
dell'Orio 1501

☎ 721 901

🚊 Vaporetto San Stae

Open: Thu–Tue lunch and
dinner

No credit cards accepted

Great bar/trattoria with a long list of both Venetian and Tuscan wines and some unusual items in among the food offerings, such as risotto with bacon and creamed eggs. It's in a good location for lunch in a quiet tree-shaded *campo*, and makes a great place to sit drinking wine with the locals in the evening. Not many visitors make it here.

Minibar da Lele

Campo dei Tolentini 183

☎ None available

🚊 Vaporetto Piazzale Roma

Open: Mon–Sat 0600–1400,
Mon–Fri 1630–2000

No credit cards accepted

A tiny Venetian institution, little more than a shack, but if you want an inexpensive drink or sandwich close to the bus station then head here, a place that commuters into Venice know about but few tourists. It serves filled sandwiches, as well as nibbles such as crisps, and in addition to soft drinks has a range of wines available by the glass, as unlikely as this seems at first glance.

Old Well Pub

Corte Canal 656

☎ 524 2760

🚊 Vaporetto Piazzale Roma

Open: Tue–Sun lunchtime
and evening, till 0200

No credit cards accepted

A great mix of a place which combines a pub and pizza parlour with some more elaborate dishes, all squeezed into a room done out as an Italian *campo*, complete with washing hanging

MENÙ - TURISTICO
LASAGNE AL-FORNO o
MACCHERONI AL RAGÙ o
SPAGHETTI - AL-POMODORO
BISTECCA-AiFERRi-MiLANESE o
POLLO-ARROSTO-con-CONTORNO
COPERTO E SERVIZIO COMPRESO
£16:000

out to dry. The menu runs to fifteen pages and the bar area has almost as long a list of cocktails and beers, especially Scottish beers.

Osteria Ai Postali ⑭

Fondamenta Rio Marin 821

☎ 715 156

🚤 Vaporetto San Toma

Open: Mon–Sat lunch and dinner

No credit cards accepted

Snacks and drinks by the canal are what's on offer here, as well as the amiably eccentric atmosphere created by the amiably eccentric owner, which means that something's always happening. It's popular with youngsters for its cheap and cheerful

nature. Try the crêpes, or *bruschette* (toasted bread with different toppings).

Alla Rivetta ⑮

Calle Sechera 637A

☎ 718 111

🚤 Vaporetto Piazzale Roma

Open: Mon–Sat 0730–2100

No credit cards accepted

A great and ancient bar with its marble counter, opera usually pumps out over the loudspeakers. Its customers are mostly locals calling in for a chat and a glass of Prosecco or one of the other local wines – your chance to try something new, very cheaply. Bar snacks are available, too, if you want something simple but tasty and filling.

Ai Vecio Fritoin ⑯

Calle della Regina 2262

☎ 522 2881

🚤 Vaporetto San Stae

Open: Tue–Sat 0930–2130

No credit cards accepted

A *fritoin* was a Venetian street stall or *osteria* that served fried fish and seafood to take away, wrapped in paper like British fish and chips. This osteria is one of the very few that maintains the tradition: ask for a *frito en scartoso* (fried fish in a paper wrap). Alternatively, stay and have a glass of Prosecco, a bar snack or even a full meal, such as fillet of sea bass baked in the oven.

SANTA CROCE
Shops, markets and picnic sites

Shops

La Boutique del Dolce ⑰

Fondamenta Garzotti Rio Maria 890

✆ 718 523

🚢 Vaporetto Riva di Biasio

Open: Thu–Tue

No credit cards accepted

Wonderful fruit tarts in the window display draw your eye to this aptly named shop, which also goes by the name of 'Gilda Vio'. There are other tempting pastries too, such as *crostata di cioccolato*, whole slabs of tiramisu, and plum cakes, as well as other smaller cakes and pastries available inside.

Calle Larga ⑱

🚢 Vaporetto San Stae

This small street that runs north from the Campo San Giacomo dell'Orio (*see below*) is the one to seek out if you're looking to have a picnic lunch in the *campo*. It has several small but high-quality delicatessens, a bakery, pastry shops, and general food stores selling filled rolls and sandwiches if you just want something cheap and filling.

Franceschini Aldo ⑲

Cristo C. Chiesa 2126

✆ 301 8969

🚢 Vaporetto San Stae

Open: Mon–Sat

No credit cards accepted

An excellent little backstreet grocery/wine shop, which has a counter displaying hams, cheeses, olives, pastas and readymade picnic dishes such as rice salad or marinated shrimps. Around the shelves are pre-packed pastas, an excellent selection of bottled and canned beers, plus a good range of wines including some very cheap half bottles.

La Margherita ⑳

Campo San Cassiano 2345

✆ 723 120

🚢 Vaporetto Rialto

Open: daily

💳 🆅🅸🆂🅰 American Express

The one-woman ceramic workshop of Margherita Rossetto is a tiny treasure trove if you are looking for colourful original kitchenware, which you can watch the owner making at her small potter's wheel in the corner of the shop. There are lots of handmade eggcups in bright yellows and blues, along with butter

dishes, milk jugs, teapots, storage jars and huge plates decorated with a motif of a bunch of grapes.

Picnic sites

Campo Nazario Sauro ㉑

🚢 Vaporetto Ferrovia

A peaceful square in this peaceful corner of Venice, the *campo* has just one café and a handful of benches where you can relax in the shade of some trees and watch the world go by ... though not much of it goes by here.

Campo San Giacomo dell'Orio ㉒

🚢 Vaporetto San Stae

This big and quiet *campo* is off the usual tourist trail, and has plenty of benches beneath shady trees if you want a break from tramping the streets. You could stock up with goodies along nearby Calle Larga (*see above*), and afterwards have a coffee or a drink in one of the lively cafés that surround the *campo*. There are restaurants too if you change your mind about the picnic, with the **Capitan Uncino** *(see page 72)* being especially good.

Campo San Simeon Profeta ㉓

🚤 Vaporetto Ferrovia

This must be one of the best-hidden picnic spots in the city, and just a stone's throw from the busy railway station. From the station cross the big bridge by the Ferrovia vaporetto stop, take the third left and turn left again to find yourself in a cul-de-sac which goes down to the edge of the Grand Canal with a nice view of some flower-bedecked modern buildings opposite. There are several benches to rest on, shaded by trees, and your only companions will probably be young children playing or old men chatting, undisturbed by Venice's main transport hub across the canal.

Giardino Papadopoli ㉔

🚤 Vaporetto Ferrovia
Open: daily 0800–1930

If you want a last peaceful picnic before taking the bus to the airport, this shady park – sizeable for Venice – is just the place, reached by taking one of the bridges in front of the bus station and heading for the trees. There are pathways and benches, and a children's playground too – a much pleasanter reminder of the city than the bustle of the bus station. It's only a short walk from the train station too, by crossing the bridge and turning right.

Grappa

Firing the soul

If you have not tried grappa before, then you should at least be prepared to try a glass of it after one of your meals in Venice. For many people one glass will be enough, as grappa is strong and can be harsh and fierce, an acquired taste that you may not feel worth the effort of acquiring. If you think you are in for a smooth scotch or brandy, think again. The word **'firewater'** was never more appropriate, but it is only fair to say that there are many smoother and more superior versions of grappa than the average glass you will find served in a bar. If you do become

a grappaholic, you can look forward to sampling lots of different flavours, and grappas that are made from different grape varieties.

Grappa is made from the sediment left over after the pressing of the grapes. This is first left to mature for several weeks, and then heated in order to drive off the alcoholic vapour. It is then cooled and the resulting liquid is a clear grappa. Most manufacturers will take the remnants of several different grape varieties from which to produce their grappa, but a superior product can be made by

taking the left-overs from a single grape variety, such as Chardonnay or Sauvignon, and producing a smoother and naturally more expensive drink. In other cases the grappa can be blended with lemon or other fruit flavours such as strawberries, raspberries, pears and apricots, to take the rough edge off the taste.

In many of the food and wine shops listed in this book you will find a range of grappas for sale, in bottles that vary as much in style as does the drink itself. Some of the more elegant bottles do make wonderful gifts. Look for the name of **Nonino**, a distillery in the town of Friuli which has been making grappa for almost a century now, and which produces some excellent single-grape varieties as well as fruit flavours, and is renowned for the striking nature of the bottles used, some of which are hand-blown on Murano.

Grappa comes originally from the town of **Bassano del Grappa** to the northwest of Venice, at the foot of Monte Grappa in the pre-Alps, from which it takes its name. There is some confusion about the derivation of the name 'grappa', for the liqueur. Some say it came from the town as that was where it was first made, others that it is a corruption of the Italian word *graspa*, which describes the dregs left in the vats after the wine-making process, from which grappa is distilled.

> **Grappa can be blended with lemon or other fruit flavours such as strawberries, raspberries, pears and apricots, to take the rough edge off the taste.**

Whatever the derivation, Bassano del Grappa is a lovely town, well worth a visit if you have some time in the area. Spanning the Brenta River is a beautifully simple 16th-century wooden bridge, the Ponte degli Alpini, though sadly the original was destroyed by the retreating German troops near the end of the Second World War, and what is there today is a faithful reproduction of the original.

Right on the bridge is the **Bottega Nardini**, named after the family which has been making grappa here since 1779, and continues to make it today. There can be no more suitable place to taste or to take away a bottle of the fiery local liquor than in this historic Bottega. You would be following the example of boatmen over the centuries, who would stop off here for a grappa while floating wood down the river to Venice to build its canals, houses and palaces.

Grappa was produced in the mountainous north of Italy as a source of warmth and comfort for workers. They would traditionally rinse out their breakfast coffee cup with a slug of grappa before going to the fields in winter, and even children would be given a swig before they set off for school on winter mornings. So when you're drinking grappa, you're drinking down a bit of local history with it.

Dorsoduro

Dorsoduro attracts visitors across the Grand Canal to see two of Venice's big attractions, the Accademia and the Peggy Guggenheim Museum. Go beyond these, though, and there's an attractive neighbourhood of relaxing squares, good restaurants, and late-night bars.

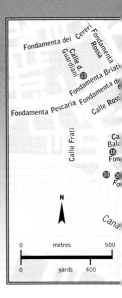

DORSODURO
Restaurants

Agli Alboretti ❶

Rio Terrà Antonio Foscarini 882

✆ 523 0058

🛥 Vaporetto Accademia

Open: Fri–Tue lunch and dinner, and Thu dinner

Reservations recommended

All credit cards accepted

International

€€

This unpretentious place, with a garden out back, serves top quality food in unusual combinations, such as small fillets of veal with dill and nettle shoots, or lamb chops with mint and blueberries.

Antica Locanda Montin ❷

Fondamenta Borgo 1147

✆ 522 7151

🛥 Vaporetto Accademia

Open: Thu–Mon lunch and dinner, and Tue lunch

Reservations recommended

All credit cards accepted

International

€€

An ancient restaurant where they welcome you like an old friend, even on your first visit. There are some tables in the garden courtyard, and dishes such as asparagus in olive oil or beef fillet cooked in brandy.

Antico Capon ❸

Campo Santa Margherita 3004

✆ 528 5252

🛥 Vaporetto Ca' Rezzonico

Open: daily lunch and dinner

Reservations unnecessary

Italian

€€

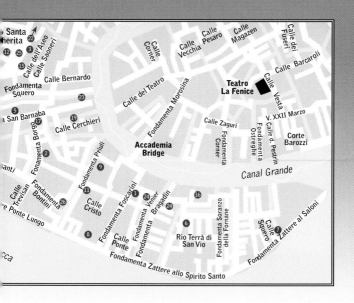

This popular place on a busy *campo* is best for a simple Mediterranean outdoor meal. The menu includes many Venetian dishes, plus pizzas, fish risotto or escalope with mushrooms in lemon juice and marsala.

Ai Cugnai ④

Piscina del Forner 857

✆ 528 9238

🚤 Vaporetto Accademia

Open: Tue–Sun lunch and dinner, closed Jan

Reservations recommended

All credit cards accepted

Venetian

€€

A charming place that's like a piece of history, tucked away near the

Accademia. The lovely, friendly female owner greets you, and the menu covers meat and fish but the fish soup is renowned, as is their spaghetti with squid.

La Furatola ⑤

Calle Lunga San Barnaba 2870A

✆ 520 8594

🚤 Vaporetto Accademia

Open: Fri–Tue lunch and dinner, closed July–Aug

Reservations recommended

All credit cards accepted

Seafood

€€€

An excellent small seafood restaurant in a

▲ Contemplating the Grand Canal

▲ The Grand Canal and the Guggenheim Museum

300-year-old building, with friendly service and a simple menu. If you want fresh fish the day's choice will be brought to you, and your selection will be cooked then expertly filleted for you at the table.

Ai Gondolieri ⑥

Ponte del Formager, San Vio 366

✆ 528 6396

🕜 Vaporetto Accademia
Open: Wed–Mon lunch and dinner
Reservations essential
All credit cards accepted
Venetian
❸❸❸

This is that rare thing in Venice, a restaurant that doesn't serve fish but appeals to meat-lovers and vegetarians equally. One speciality in this cosy but expensive place is risotto *al radicchio* (with chicory). Game is good in season.

Linea d'Ombra ⑦

Fondamenta delle Zattere 19
✆ 528 5259
🚤 Vaporetto Salute
Open: Thu–Tue lunch and dinner, except closed Sun dinner
Reservations unnecessary
All credit cards accepted
Venetian
€€

As far east on the southern side of Dorsoduro as you can go, with a terrific view across to Giudecca, this casual eating place has all the Venetian specialities: squid cooked in its own ink, risotto and fresh fish.

Ristorante alla Zattere ⑧

Fondamenta Zattere ai Gesuiti 795
✆ 520 4224
🚤 Vaporetto Zattere
Open: Wed–Mon lunch and dinner, closed Nov
Reservations recommended
💳 💳
Venetian
€€

This informal restaurant has a wonderful view across to Giudecca, as well as Venetian dishes such as squid cooked in its own ink and served with polenta. It also does excellent and inexpensive pizzas.

Taverna San Trovaso ⑨

Fondamenta Priuli 1016
✆ 520 3703
🚤 Vaporetto Accademia
Open: Tue–Sun, lunch and dinner
Reservations recommended
All credit cards accepted
Italian
€€

Tripe with tomato sauce and polenta, duck breast with a mushroom and cream sauce or grilled eel with polenta are among the more adventurous options in this trattoria-pizzeria.

Trattoria San Basilio ⑩

Calle del Vento 1516
✆ 521 0028
🚤 Vaporetto San Basilio
Open: Mon–Sat lunch and dinner
Reservations unnecessary
All credit cards accepted
Venetian
€€

Simple eating place with great views of Giudecca, and a menu that runs through the Venetian specialities: spaghetti with squid, spaghetti with clams, mixed fried fish or, more unusually, a fish lasagne.

Taverna San Tr
Ristorante Pizzeria
Dorso Duro 1016 (VE) - Tel. 041.52.03.703 - Fax
Aria Condizionata - Air Conditioned - Klim
Chiuso Lunedi' - Close Monday - Montags geschlosse
Orario: 12.00 - 14.50 / 19.00 - 21.50

Primi Piatti

peisen	First course - Premier Plàtes - Erster Gang	
	Zuppa di verdura Vegetable soup Potage aux légumes Gemüsesuppe	L. 10.000
L. 10.000	Zuppa di pesce Fish soup Soupe de poisson Fischsuppe	L. 15.000
	Lasagne al forno Creamy baked noodles Lasagnes au gratin Ueberbackene Bandnudeln	L. 10.000
L. 10.000	Rigatoni all'amatriciana (pancetta,cipolla,pomodoro) Rigatoni with bacon, onions, and tomato sauce Rigatoni aux sauce tomate as lard Rigatoni mit Speck, Tomatensauce	L. 10.000
	Rigatoni alla San Trovaso (pomodoro,panna,piselli) Rigatoni with green peas, tomato sauce, and creme sauce Rigatoni aux petit-pois, sauce tomate, crème Rigatoni mit Erbsen, Tomatensauce, Sahne	L. 10.000
L. 15.000	Tortelloni alla primavera (panna,prosciutto,piselli) Tortelloni with ham, green peas and cream sauce Tortelloni aux petit- pois, jambon, crème Tortelloni mit Schinken, Erbsen	L. 10.000
	Spaghetti alla carbonara Spaghetti with beaten eggs and diced browned bacon	L. 10.000

▲ Taverna San Trovaso

DORSODURO
Bars, cafés and pubs

Al Bottegon ⑪

Fondamenta Nani 992

✆ 523 0034

🚤 Vaporetto Zaccere

Open: Mon–Sat lunch and dinner and Sun lunch

No credit cards accepted

One of the best of the city's *bacari*, this unassuming-looking place doubles as wine shop (*see page 84*) and bar. It is family run and usually packed with regulars, sampling from a huge wine list or nibbling on simple cold snacks such as salami or cheese.

Il Caffè ⑫

Campo Santa Margherita 2963

✆ 528 7998

🚤 Vaporetto Ca' Rezzonico

Open: Mon–Sat

No credit cards accepted

Bohemian bar that barely closes, except for a break on Sunday, so is the place to go if you want a late-night drink or early breakfast. It appeals to the local students and artists, and is noisy but has character.

Da Codroma ⑬

Ponte del Soccorso 2540

✆ 524 6789

🚤 Vaporetto San Basilio

Open: daily lunch and dinner, all day Sat–Sun, closed Mon dinner

No credit cards accepted

▲ Il Caffè

Great location on a canal and right by a bridge for this traditional *bacaro* that has been here for over 300 years – and looks it, from the ancient interior and the fact that everyone seems to be a regular. There's wine, snacks and occasional live music and other events.

Dolce Vita 14

Rio Terrà della Scoazzera 2894A

✆ 523 1115

🚤 Vaporetto Ca' Rezzonico

Open: Mon–Sat lunchtime and evenings till 0200

This American bar is the place to head for, just off the Campo Santa Margherita, if you're missing that Martini, or fancy a Tequila Sunrise or other cocktail. It also has a good line in beers, including Bud of course, and can rustle up anything from a club sandwich to a full meal.

Margaret DuChamp 15

Campo Santa Margherita 3019

✆ 528 6255

🚤 Vaporetto Ca' Rezzonico

Open: daily

No credit cards accepted

This fashionable hangout, with tables outside on one of the city's liveliest *campos*, also has indoor seating in a modern-looking bar which serves up several draught beers, as well as snacks and coffees.

Peggy Guggenheim Collection Café 16

Calle San Cristoforo 701

✆ 520 6288

🚤 Vaporetto Accademia

Open: Wed–Mon, museum hours

No credit cards accepted

This smart new café is better than the average museum outlet as its menu is the responsibility of the superb **Ai Gondolieri** kitchens nearby (*see page 79*). There are the usual snacks and salads, or relax with a coffee or a glass of wine as a break from one of the city's most interesting art collections.

Al Quattro Ferri 17

Calle Lunga San Barnaba 2754

✆ 520 6978

🚤 Vaporetto Ca' Rezzonico

Open: Mon–Sat lunch and dinner

No credit cards accepted

This newish wine bar-*bacari* already appears to have been here for years, and its owners try to make sure that there are both good cheap wines and more expensive options for the discerning palate. A good range of bar snacks too.

Da Sandro 17

Calle Lunga San Barnaba 2753A

✆ 523 0531

🚤 Vaporetto Accademia

Open: Tue–Sat lunch and dinner and Sun lunch

No credit cards accepted

This wine bar-*osteria* looks nothing much from the outside, but inside its chic and smart look is enhanced by lots of greenery. Wine predominates, especially from the Veneto, but you can also eat simple dishes such as fried meat croquettes.

Da Toni 18

Fondamenta San Basilio 1642

✆ 528 6899

🚤 Vaporetto San Basilio

Open: Tue–Sun all day, closed Christmas and three weeks in Aug/Sep

No credit cards accepted

This old bar-trattoria will serve you a full meal if you wish, or you can just join the local people inside or by the canal outside, enjoying the atmosphere and the conversation, and the range of wines and beers available.

Vini Padovani 19

Calle Cerchieri 1280

✆ 523 6370

🚤 Vaporetto Ca' Rezzonico

Open: Mon–Sat till 2100

No credit cards accepted

There's a good choice of wines in a setting that combines the old tradition of the long-standing inn with the new approach of young owners. The food stays simple, such as *crostini*, sausage and mushroom, salami and polenta.

DORSODURO
Shops, markets and picnic sites

Shops

Bilia 🔟20

Fondamente delle Zattere 1491

☎ 522 6187

🚤 Vaporetto San Basilio

Open: daily

No credit cards accepted

Only a supermarket but worth mentioning as it is open every day, so if only here for a weekend you can visit on a Sunday before heading home and stock up with wines, kitchen spices, and very cheap pastas, dried mushrooms, sun-dried tomatoes, olives and other goodies.

Al Bottegon 1️⃣1️⃣

Fondamenta Nani 992

☎ 523 0034

🚤 Vaporetto Zaccere

Open: Mon–Sat lunch and dinner and Sun lunch

No credit cards accepted

Already listed as a bar (see page 82), this deserves another entry to make sure you visit it, as it is also one of the best-stocked little wine shops in Venice. One entire long wall opposite the bar is lined with Italian wines, and whatever you want to try is probably here. You can also sample a good range at the bar,

before buying a bottle to take away.

Camilla 2️⃣1️⃣

Campo dei Carmini 2609

☎ 523 5277

🚤 Vaporetto Ca' Rezzonico

Open: Tue–Sat

No credit cards accepted

A charming little ceramics shop stocking only work by the owner. Most items are decorative pieces but there are also some lovely plates, dishes and bowls in bright Mediterranean colours that would cheer up any table or kitchen.

La Ciotola 2️⃣2️⃣

Calle P. Crosera 3948

☎ 526 6127

🚤 Vaporetto San Toma

Open: Mon–Sat, closed lunchtime

💳

Check out these up-market ceramics made by the owners (who also run pottery courses). Among the kitchenware and tableware are cups and plates, and the styles range from ultra-modern and simple to others with traditional Venetian designs.

Genninger Studio 2️⃣3️⃣

Calle dei Traghetto 2793A

☎ 522 5565

🚤 Vaporetto Ca' Rezzonico

Open: Mon–Sat, closed lunchtime

💳 American Express

A stylish glass shop in great contrast to much of the identikit and garish Murano glass on offer. Here instead are engraved wine goblets and brandy glasses, exquisite little liqueur glasses, candles for the table, all elaborately decorated, so not a place to come if your tastes are simple ... or cheap.

Sent – San Vio 2️⃣4️⃣

Campo San Vio 669

☎ 520 8136

🚤 Vaporetto Accademia

Open: Mon, Wed–Sat

All credit cards accepted

An arty glass shop with very few objects but very stylish ones, displayed in reverential museum-style. Many are vases and plates, in simple, delicate colours, so worth seeing if you are visiting the nearby Accademia.

Picnic sites	

Campo San Barnaba 5️⃣

🚤 Vaporetto Ca' Rezzonico

Open: market Mon–Sat

The grocery barges on the nearby canal are an

unusual sight to seze, laden down with colourful fruit and veg. The *campo* is a busy little square, and although it has no benches there is an old well in the centre to sit by, and a couple of cafés if you want a drink to go with your picnic.

Campo Santa Margherita

🚤 Vaporetto Ca' Rezzonico

Open: market Mon–Sat

This busy *campo* has several sets of benches,

including a cluster of them under some trees, some with small tables beside them. There is also a public WC, and the square has a drinking fountain and is surrounded by cafés if you want a drink to round off your picnic.

Campo Trovaso 26

🚤 Vaporetto Zattere

One of the few patches of green in Venice where you can enjoy sitting on a bench and looking out over a quiet

canal, and right beside you is one of the last remaining gondola boatyards in the city.

Fondamenta delle Zattere 27

🚤 Vaporetto San Basilio

If you want a picnic with a view, here is a fine one right across the water to Giudecca. There are benches and tables, under an awning, and a public toilet nearby too.

▲ Campo San Margherita

The best ice cream

Glorious gelati

Italy is synonymous with good ice cream (*gelato*), and Venice with its numerous tourists is especially well supplied with ice-cream shops. If you don't want a full dessert with a meal, or simply want to save a little money, wander in any direction from the restaurant and you won't have to walk far before you come across a rainbow display of ice creams. The only problem you face is how to choose from the many flavours on offer.

Whichever you choose, you can be sure that you will be getting one of the most delicious ice creams in the world. Italian ice cream is made from eggs, milk, sugar and totally natural flavours, with fresh fruit and some sugar being used in the

fruit flavours. The result is a texture and taste that puts the majority of commercial ice-cream brands to shame, being rich, creamy, light and actually tasting of what it is meant to taste of, not some synthetic substitute. *Gelato* has an equally rich history, its invention credited to a man named **Bernardo Buontalenti** in 1565 for the Medici family.

You can buy the ice cream in cones, usually with one, two or three scoops, and you can mix any flavours you like. You can also buy tubs in various sizes, usually indicated by diagrams behind the counter, and again with a number of scoops in them. These are much easier to eat, although there is a certain amount of fun to be had in trying to finish a full cone before the ice cream starts melting and dripping down your hand. You might even want to buy more than a tub will hold, and take away a selection of flavours in a larger container, as you will see many locals doing, and taking them home to round off a meal.

One thing to note is that while all the ice-cream displays look alike, with their two rows of flavours in their stainless-steel containers (plastic containers indicate mass-produced *gelato*), they are not all the same. Some do have flavours that the others don't have, and the author's particular favourite is *panna*

cotta, from an ice-cream shop on the Campo San Rocco. Tiramisu is another delight, which most places have, and while there is usually a visual aid along with the name in Italian, a translation of some of the more unusual flavours is given below.

So where is the best place to buy ice cream in Venice? The obvious answer is the nearest place, when the urge strikes, but there are a few ice-cream stores which locals rate as the best, and it shouldn't be too arduous a chore to do a comparison taste to see if you agree. The number one name is **Paolin** (*Campo San Stefano 2962A; ☎ 522 5576; ⊙ vaporetto Santa Maria del Giglio; open: daily*). This may actually have more to do with the pleasant location on an attractive *campo*, than for its historical associations – Paolin is credited as being the oldest ice-cream parlour in Venice, having been here since the 1930s. However, there is no disputing the fine quality, whether you eat it in the café, which also serves drinks and other eats, or take it away with you.

Another favourite is **Gelateria Nico** (*Zattere 922; ☎ 522 5293; ⊙ vaporetto Zattere; open: Fri–Wed, closed late Dec–late Jan*). Again, the setting helps, this ice-cream shop/café with outdoor seating looking out towards Giudecca, but the homemade ice cream is also superb.

> ... there is a certain amount of fun to be had in trying to finish a full cone before the ice-cream starts melting and dripping down your hand ...

ICE-CREAM FLAVOURS

albicocca – apricot
amarena – sour cherry
ananas – pineapple
anguria – watermelon
arancia – orange
caco – persimmon, also *diaspora*
castagna – chestnut
ciliega – cherry
cocco – coconut
crema – custard made from egg yolks
datteri – date
fico – fig
fragola – strawberry
fragoline – wild strawberry
frutti di bosco – wild berries/fruits of the forest
lampone – raspberry
macedonia – fruit salad
malaga – raisin
mela – apple
menta – mint
mirtillo – blueberry
more – blackberry
nespola – medlar
nocciola – hazelnut
noce – walnut
panna – whipped cream
pera – pear
pesca – peach
pescanoce – nectarine
pompelmo – grapefruit
ribes – blackcurrant or redcurrant
riso – rice pudding
stracciatella – chocolate chip
stracciatella di menta – mint chocolate chip
tarocchio – blood orange
torroncino – nougat
uva – grape
vaniglia – vanilla
zuppa inglese – trifle

Food etiquette and culture

FINDING YOUR WAY AROUND

Please use the maps in this book, perhaps in combination with an indexed street map. Never simply use an address to find a restaurant, as there are many street names which are repeated several times throughout the city, sometimes even close to each other in the same area.

All establishments will have a number, though this does not quite equate to the street numbers which most cities have. The houses along a street or around a square will be numbered consecutively ... until you come to a gap and then the next number may be totally out of sequence. The numbers are a cross between a street number and a zip/postal code, and there is a logic to their distribution, but if you only have an incomplete address (that is, just a district and a number with no street name to go with it), then it could take a long time to find the right place.

WHEN TO EAT

If you want to be truly Venetian, you will eat all day long. Breakfast is served from about 0700 until 1030, and is almost immediately followed by a snack of a sandwich, a pastry and more coffee. Lunch will follow starting at about 1230 or 1300, and while many places will start to quieten down at about 1500, there are plenty that will still be lively thanks to the late lunchers.

After a gap for a siesta, it will be time in the early evening for an *ombra*, or glass of wine, accompanied by *cicchetti*, which are bar snacks like the Spanish *tapas*. You could dine entirely on these if you wish, though some of the places serving them will close by about 2000 or 2030 (while others go on all night). This is the time when many Venetians then move on to the restaurant of their choice, but visitors who wish to eat earlier will find them open from about 1900 onwards.

THE MENU

Venetian menus are like those in the rest of Italy, made up of several courses. You don't have to have something from each course, and if you just want a light meal it is perfectly fine to have only a pasta dish or a main course.

The menu begins with the *salumi*, or appetiser, followed by an *antipasto*. This is the pre-pasta or starter course. This is followed by the *primo*, or first course, which will usually be either soup or a kind of pasta. The *secondo* or second course will be the meat or fish course, which differs from some food cultures where a fish course might be followed by a meat course.

After the *secondo* you might have a *contorno*, or salad course, though you can also have the salad as a starter or with your main course if you wish. You would then have the *formaggio* or cheese course before your dessert, the *dolce*, followed by coffee and finally a glass of grappa or liqueur. Note that Italians almost always drink espresso after a meal. Cappuccino is a breakfast drink, but no one will bat an eyelid if you ask for one after a meal, as they are used to the strange habits of tourists.

BREAKFAST

Most hotels will offer you a continental breakfast, and you will be asked if you want to drink tea, coffee or hot chocolate. Coffee may come black unless you ask for *latte*, milk, but note that a *caffè latte* is made with the milk already mixed into it. The typical Italian breakfast drink is cappuccino, but not many hotels offer this as it takes time to make.

To eat you will be offered rolls, croissants and perhaps toast, although it will be the dried toast popular on the continent, not

toasted bread. You will also get butter and preserves, and in smarter hotels perhaps also some cold meats and cheeses.

TIPPING

By law all restaurant bills must include a service charge, which should be shown on the bill. In fact it is illegal not to provide a detailed bill to the customer. The amount of the service charge varies from restaurant to restaurant, usually between 10 and 15 per cent. The amount of your tip depends on the amount of the service charge and the standard of the service. If you have already paid 15 per cent on your bill, then you would probably only leave a nominal amount as a tip. If the service charge is low, say 10 per cent, and service has been good, you might want to leave another 10 per cent as a tip.

Some waiters in the more touristy places will, if asked about the service charge, tell you that it goes to the restaurant and not to the waiter. That is precisely when *not* to tip. Although Venice is almost sinking beneath the weight of visitors, and that does mean there are inevitably some tourist traps, the places listed in this guide are serving good food at fair prices, at the time of writing.

Menu decoder

MEALS
colazione – breakfast
pranzo – lunch
cena – dinner
merenda – snack
panino – sandwich, also *tramezzino*
piatto unico – one-course meal
porzione – portion

GENERAL TERMS
antipasto misto – mixed appetisers
bichiere – glass
bottiglia – bottle
burro – butter
caldo – hot
cavatappi – corkscrew
coltello – knife
congelato – frozen
conto – bill
coperto – cover charge

coppa – cup
crudo – raw
cucchiaio – spoon
fegato – slice
filetto – fillet
forchetta – fork
freddo – cold
panna – cream
piatto – plate
piatto del giorno – dish of the day
sale – salt
senapo – mustard
servizzio – service charge
tovagliolo – napkin
zucherro – sugar

COOKING METHODS
affumicato – smoked
arrosto – roast
ben cotto – well-done (for cooking meat)

brasata – braised
al forno – baked
fritto – fried
fuso – melted
alla griglia – grilled
lesso – boiled
al puntino – medium (for cooking meat)
ripieno – stuffed
al sangue – rare (for cooking meat)
stufato – braised or stewed
al vapore – steamed

DRESSINGS AND SAUCES
aceto – vinegar
aceto balsamico – balsamic vinegar
besclamellé – béchamel sauce
olio d'oliva – olive oil
ragu – meat sauce
tocco/tucco – sauce, also *sugo*

BREADS
bruschetta – garlic bread
cornetti – croissants
foccacia – a flat bread, like the base of a pizza
grissini – breadsticks
pane – bread
panino – bread roll

STARTERS AND SUNDRY DISHES
brodo – broth
caponata – aubergine/eggplant salad, with olives and tomatoes
crocchette – croquettes
crostini – a canapé, often with paté
fritto misto – mixed fried dish
gnocchi – potato dumplings
insaccati – sausage and salami
insalata – salad
minestra – soup, also *zuppa*
polpettone – meatloaf
pure – mashed/creamed potatoes

PASTA DISHES
agnolotti – pasta stuffed with meat, egg and cheese
bigoli – pasta made in a particular kind of press
cappelletti – stuffed pasta
fusilli – short length of pasta
maccheroni – macaroni
pasta corta – refers to short lengths of pasta, such as *penne*
penne – a quill-shaped pasta
sfoglia – a sheet of pasta which is cut into noodles or filled with different ingredients
tagliatelle – pasta rich in eggs and made in flat strips
tortellini – pasta rich in eggs, made into rings and usually stuffed

FISH AND SEAFOOD
acciughe – anchovies, also *alici*
aragosta – lobster, also *astice*
arsella – clam
baccala – dried salt cod
branzino – sea bass, also *spigola*
burrida – fish stew
calamari – squid
capesante – scallops
cozze – mussels
crostacei – shellfish
gamberi – prawns
granchio – crab
merluzzo – cod
ostriche – oysters
pesce – fish
polpo – octopus
sarde – sardines
sogliola – sole
tonno – tuna
trota – trout

MEAT DISHES
agnello – lamb
anatra – duck
bistecca – beefsteak

bresaola – beef that has been cured and dried and then sliced thinly
cacciagione – game
capriolo – venison
carne – meat
carpaccio – thinly sliced raw beef (see recipes)
cinghiale – wild boar
colomba – wood pigeon
coniglio – rabbit
controfiletto – sirloin steak
cotechino – pork sausage
fagiano – pheasant
fegato – calf's liver
maiale – pork
manzo – beef
ossobucco – shin of veal
pancetta – salt-cured bacon
pollo – chicken
polpette – meatballs
il prosciutto cotto – cooked ham; *crudo* is cured
salsiccia – sausage
scaloppine – escalopes
selvaggina – game
vitello – veal

HERBS, NUTS, PULSES AND VEGETABLES
aglio – garlic
asparagi – asparagus
barbabietola – beetroot
capperi – capers

carciofi – artichokes
carote – carrots
cavolo – cabbage
la cipolla – onion
erbe – herbs
fagioli – beans
funghi – mushrooms
lattuga – lettuce
lenticchie – lentils
melanzana – aubergine/eggplant
menta – mint
patate – potatoes
patatine fritte – French fries/ chips
pepe – pepper
peperoncini – chilli pepper
peperoni – bell peppers
piselli – peas
pomodoro – tomato
porcini – mushroom
porri – leeks
riso – rice
sedano – celery
spinaci – spinach
tartufi – truffles
verdure – vegetables
zenzero – ginger

FRUIT
banane – bananas
ginepro – juniper berries
limone – lemon
marroni – chestnuts
melacotogna – quince

melagrana – pomegranate
melone – melon
oliva – olive
prugna – plum, also *susina*
rabarbaro – rhubarb
tarocco – blood orange

See page 87 for further fruits

DESSERTS AND CHEESE

baci di dama – chocolate-covered
  almond biscuits
bel paese – a mild-tasting soft
  cheese
biscotti – biscuits
cioccolata – chocolate
crema – custard
crostata – fruit tart
frutta cotta – fruit cooked in
  wine and spices
gorgonzola dolce – a slightly
  milder version of the blue
  gorgonzola cheese
latte fritto – literally 'fried milk',
  it is a cinnamon-flavoured
  custard dessert
mascarpone – rich, sweet triple-
  cream cheese
panna cotta – creamy dessert, like
  a crème caramel
parmigiano – parmesan cheese
semifreddo – an ice cream with
  whipped cream folded into it
sorbetto – sorbet
tiramisu – creamy dessert made
  from mascarpone, espresso
  coffee and chocolate (the
  name literally means 'pick-
  me-up')
torrone – rich nougat dessert
  made with hazelnuts, egg
  whites and either sugar or
  honey
torta – cake
zabbaione/zabbaglioni – egg
  yolks whipped with sugar and
  some wine to make a tangy,
  frothy dessert

DRINKS

acqua del rubinetto – tap water
acqua minerale – mineral water
  (*gassata* – sparkling, *naturale*
  – still)
alla spina – on draught (of beer)
amabile – semi-sweet (of wines)
analcolico – non-alcoholic
aperitivo – aperitif
aranciata – fizzy orange drink
bianco – white
birra – beer
caffè – coffee (usually taken to
  mean an espresso)
caffè latte – large coffee made
  with milk
caffè macchiato – espresso with a
  dash of milk
caldo – hot
cioccolata calde – hot chocolate
ghiaccio – ice
granita – water/ice with
  flavouring
liscio – neat, as opposed to 'on
  the rocks'
lista dei vini – the wine list
rosso – red
seltz – soda water
spremuta di arancia – freshly-
  squeezed orange juice
succo di frutta – fruit juice
thè/tè – tea
tisana – herbal tea
vino – wine
vino da tavola – table wine
vino della casa – house wine

Venetian cuisine

Venetian cuisine is influenced
by the city's historic trading
links with the Orient. Rice,
polenta, beans and salt cod
are transformed into exotic,
refined dishes. Pasta is seldom
used, except for *gnocchi*.

Recipes

Sardines in saor
(sardelle in saor)

This dish probably appears on almost as many Venetian restaurant menus as tiramisu (which was invented in Treviso), and in as many variations. By varying the amounts of onions, wine or vinegar you can experiment to produce a blend that you prefer. It is a dish that shows how you can combine the simplest local ingredients, all widely available, to produce a delicious combination ... and it is totally Venetian.

Serves 4–6

INGREDIENTS

2lb sardines
1lb onions
½ cup of flour
1 cup of olive oil
2 cups of red wine vinegar
2 tablespoons of pinenuts
2 tablespoons of raisins
salt

Gut and remove the bones and heads of the sardines. Wash them, pat them dry and then dip the sardines in the flour and shake off the excess.

Take half the olive oil and heat it in a frying pan. When it is hot, fry the sardines for a few minutes and then place them on paper towels to drain off the excess oil before salting them and putting them aside on a plate.

Slice the onions and then heat the rest of the oil in a second frying pan over a low heat, putting in the onions and cooking them till they soften and brown. Add the vinegar and continue cooking for a few more minutes to reduce the vinegar. Add some salt to the onions and vinegar, and then put the mixture to one side.

Place layers of the sardines, onions, pinenuts and raisins in a serving dish with a top on it. Cover the

dish and place in a refrigerator to marinate for 1 to 2 days before serving.

Carpaccio

Carpaccio was invented in **Harry's Bar** (*see page 9*) in Venice in 1950, the same bar where the Bellini cocktail was created in the 1930s. Carpaccio was the creation of the then owner of Harry's Bar, Giuseppe Cipriani, when one of his best customers, Contessa Amalia Nani Mocenigo, told him that her doctor had instructed her not to eat cooked meat for health reasons. Cipriani put his mind to work and came up with a dish for the contessa,

which got round the restriction. He took paper-thin slices of raw beef, which he dressed with a sauce made of lemon juice, mayonnaise, horseradish and milk.

The name came from the 16th-century painter Vittore Carpaccio whose works were being exhibited in Venice at the time and which showed off his special use of reds and whites. Cipriani thought the dish looked like one of Carpaccio's works. Other customers in Harry's Bar tried the dish and liked it, and so it entered the world's cookbooks. It is also possible to prepare a seafood carpaccio using equally thin slices of raw fish.

Serves 6

INGREDIENTS

1½ lb of trimmed shell of beef

1 teaspoon of lemon juice

¼ cup of mayonnaise

2½ tablespoons of milk

2 teaspoons of Worcestershire sauce

salt

white pepper

Put the beef in the freezer until it becomes firm and easy to cut. You will need a very sharp chef's kitchen knife to slice it into paper-thin pieces. Mix the mayonnaise, lemon juice and Worcestershire sauce. Add the milk and mix in until you have a thin sauce the consistency of which you like. Add the salt and pepper to taste. Pour the sauce over the slices of beef and serve.

Published by Thomas Cook Publishing
Thomas Cook Holdings Ltd
PO Box 227
Thorpe Wood
Peterborough PE3 6PU
United Kingdom

Telephone: 01733 503571
Email: books@thomascook.com

Text © 2001 Thomas Cook Publishing
Maps © 2001 Thomas Cook Publishing

ISBN 1 841570 92 3

Distributed in the United States of
America by the Globe Pequot Press,
PO Box 480, Guilford, Connecticut
06437, USA

Publisher: Donald Greig
Commissioning Editor: Deborah Parker
Map Editor: Bernard Horton

Project management: Dial House
    Publishing
Series Editor: Christopher Catling
Copy Editor: Lucy Thomson
Proofreader: Jan Wiltshire

Series and cover design: WhiteLight
Cover artwork: WhiteLight and
    Kaarin Wall
Text layout: SJM Design Consultancy,
    Dial House Publishing
Maps prepared by Polly Senior
    Cartography

Repro and image setting: PDQ Digital
    Media Solutions Ltd
Printed and bound in Italy by
    Eurografica SpA

Written and researched by **Mike Gerrard**

The author would like to thank **Room
Service** (✆ *070 2636 6888*) for finding him
the lovely Hotel Serenissima at a busy
time of year.

We would like to thank the author for the
photographs used in this book, to whom
the copyright belongs, with the exception
of the following:
Antico Martini (page 19)
Donna Dailey (pages 2, 10, 14, 20, 22, 25,
    40, 59, 64, 72, 79 and 80)
John Heseltine (pages 94 and 95)
Orient-Express Hotels (page 26)
Vino Vino (page 23).